P9-CBX-071

Grrr!

Celebrities

ARE RUINING OUR

COUNTRY . . . AND

OTHER REASONS

Why We're

ALL IN TROUBLE

St. Martin's Press ✹ New York

Grrr!

Celebrities

ARE RUINING OUR

COUNTRY . . . AND

OTHER REASONS

Why We're

ALL IN TROUBLE

(((. . .)))

Mike Straka

www.stmartins.com

Design by Susan Walsh

Library of Congress Cataloging-in-Publication Data

Straka, Mike.
   Grrr! Celebrities are ruining our country . . . and other reasons why we're all in trouble / Mike Straka.—1st ed.
      p.   cm.
   ISBN-13: 978-0-312-36154-9
   ISBN-10: 0-312-36154-8
   1. Popular culture—United States.   2. Political culture—United States.
3. Celebrities—United States.   4. Politicians—United States.   5. United States—Social life and customs—1971–   6. United States—Social conditions—1980–
7. United States—Politics and government—2001–   I. Fox News.   II. Title.

E169.Z83S78 2007
306.0973'09045—dc22   2006051184

First Edition: February 2007

10   9   8   7   6   5   4   3   2   1

For my girls, Emily and Maxine,
without whose love I am nothing

CONTENTS

THE Grrr! LEXICON:
A Glossary of Terms for Your Edification

Oblivion (oh-BLI-vé-un)—A person who is so oblivious to his surroundings that he abandons all common courtesy and commits daily acts of rudeness. Oblivions are oblivious to the very fact that they are Oblivions, which makes it difficult for the Oblivion to ever see the error of his ways.

Obliviot—A person whose Oblivionism is dangerous to others.

Left Lane Vigilante—An automobile driver who believes so strongly in speed limit highway laws that she will drive slower than the posted speed limit in the passing lane, forcing people to pass on the right. *These people are committed to keeping you from getting a speeding ticket, and they will do whatever it takes to keep you behind them.*

Self-Righteon—A person who is always right and has to let every one know it. These are usually self-absorbed ex-smokers, ex-drinkers, born-again Christians, and other people in love with themselves.

ImporTants—Sooo important that they can't sit through a restaurant meal without loudly talking business on the cell phone, or they believe that if they quit their job their employer's business would go down in flames.

Wal-Martians—These are grocery store Oblivions who wait until their entire cart is rung up before whipping out the checkbook. These are the folks whose families span across entire shopping aisles, debating the pros and cons of all-in-one shampoo and conditioner or stopping to chat with their next-door neighbor to catch up on the last five years.

Polignorants—People who know nothing about politics yet nod profusely and agree with the loudest people in the room—like Michael Moore or Rush Limbaugh.

Real-ities—People who are treated like celebrities even though their only contribution to society is appearing on a reality show.

Stupid Lit'l Dreamers—This is a term of endearment. When I was a page at CBS-TV, my friend Joe Long, who was also a page, would call me at whoever's phone I happened to be answering that day and disguise his voice as some media bigwig.

"Is this Mike Straka?" he'd say in an Australian accent. "This is Rupert Murdoch calling. I have your resume in front of me and—" Suddenly, he'd break into the Supertramp song "Dreamer," singing, "Dreamer, you stupid lit'l dreamer," English accent and all.

We'd laugh our butts off.

I still am that Stupid Lit'l Dreamer, but what the hell? Dream big and never let No get you down. Don't forget that no matter how many Nos you hear, it only takes one Yes to make your career.

A CRASH COURSE IN OBLIVIONISM

- On the road, they are deputized as Left Lane Vigilantes, and they diligently set the pace for all those who dare drive more than the posted speed limit.

- At restaurants, they let their kids run rampant under the misguided perception that everybody finds their little monsters as cute as they do—and they don't tip well.

- They can't spend more than ten minutes without putting the cell phone to an ear and can't seem to grasp the fact that cell phone technology is so advanced these days they no longer need to yell for the person on the other end to hear them.

- Pssst . . . excuse me, Ms. Oblivion. See this line gathered behind you at the condiments table? We'd also like to put cream and sugar in our coffee, so please take your conversation somewhere else.

- Take your barking dog inside your house. Your little pooch is causing someone to grind the enamel off his teeth.

- Commuters who ride the bus or train every day know that eventually every seat will be filled before they reach the metropolis. But commuter Oblivions insist on using the seat next to them for their bags, their coats, their coffee, whatever—and then, when someone comes along looking to sit down, they huff and puff and make a general production out of moving all their crap from the seat.

▣ In the mall, they're the ones pushing the SUV-sized strollers and taking out a chunk of your Achilles' heel without so much as a by-your-leave.

▣ On the sidewalk, they're the people with tunnel vision carelessly swinging their lit cigarettes as they walk down the block and burn everyone in their path.

▣ And, oh, it's never their fault. Never.

You probably spotted several Oblivions just while buying this book.

Grrr!

Celebrities

ARE RUINING OUR

COUNTRY . . . AND

OTHER REASONS

Why We're

ALL IN TROUBLE

$(((\ldots)))$

Introduction

Remember *The Arsenio Hall Show?*

I know it seems like a lifetime since Hall even had a career in front of the camera, but it wasn't too long ago when millions of television viewers tuned in every night to the comedian's fledgling late-night show, which quickly became a major player in the genre.

As with most success stories, Arsenio's ego got the better of him, and pretty soon the words "Arseniooooooooooooooo Hall" became a distant memory.

But one of Arsenio's segments will stand the test of time, even if its creator did not.

It was the "Things That Make Me Go Hmmmm" segment. In it, Hall posed rhetorical questions and put his finger on his chin while saying, "Hmmmmm."

"You ever wonder why express checkout lanes always take the longest to ring up your groceries? Hmmmmm."

The audience always got a kick out of that and so did I, watching TV in my college dorm room in New Brunswick, New Jersey.

When I started writing a column online I concentrated on entertainment commentary. Having worked as an actor and being an entertainment reporter, I figured my interest in and exposure to the industry, its stars, and its power players, and with a better-than-average understanding of how that business works, made me qualified to pontificate on Hollywood, TV news, and pop culture.

But I always wanted to pay homage to Arsenio and do a list of things that make me go "Hmmm." However, while constantly thinking about clever "hmmmisms," I discovered that more things actually made me go "Grrr!"—so I switched gears and made up my own list.

The list struck a chord with readers, and today it gets an average of 230,000 page views every week, and generates anywhere between 500 and 2,000 weekly e-mails, depending on the topic. The column's popularity also afforded me the opportunity to spin off into a Web-based video series, called *The Real Deal*, which has tallied millions of downloads since its inception.

The column even spawned the Grrr! Lexicon, a list of made-up terms that are really nothing more than family-friendly insults to our fellow, eh-hem, man, and terms like *Oblivion* and *Left Lane Vigilantes* have made it into some folks' daily vocabularies.

Celebrities have been frequent targets of the Grrr, but I never set out to be a celebrity basher, and even though several are named in the following pages, I don't enter into Grrring celebrities with malice.

The simple, oftentimes sad truth is celebrities are bigger Oblivions than even the most Grrring everyday morons we encounter, and that's mostly because celebrities are always surrounded by people willing to cater to their every whim. After a while they begin to expect special treatment and favors wherever they go.

I define an Oblivion as a person who is rude without even knowing he's being rude because he's simply too oblivious to his surroundings. He's got tunnel vision and only cares about his own needs.

Not every Oblivion is a celebrity, but every celebrity is an Oblivion.

Did you know that a lot of celebrities have several children out of wedlock with multiple partners? Of course you do, but we don't hear too much grumbling about it.

Why is that?

Because celebrities, including athletes, usually have enough money to financially support multiple "families," however, does that make it right? Is that enough?

Fast forward eighteen years later and you may wonder how so-and-so's daughter, whom you never heard of before is posing for *Playboy* and crying about how she was neglected by her famous parent for so many years.

Yet in the world of celebrity worship we live in, nobody really cares about how Joe Football Player or Jane Actress is destroying his or her own flesh and blood. All we care about is that they stay beautiful and keep us entertained.

So what if they're contributing to the general malaise of our society. That's more forgivable than growing old and getting fat!

Of course, the unconditional love received by celebs is never enough, so they need more attention. Put a camera in front of them, and they know whom you should vote for and what issues should be important to you.

I'll never forget watching an entertainment reporter tell viewers during the 2004 presidential election how Leonardo DiCaprio "wrote his own speech" when he was stumping for John Kerry.

Well, I hadn't planned on voting for Kerry, but since DiCaprio wrote his own speech, well then, by all means. I mean, the guy wrote his own speech!

It's laughable, but the sad fact is so many zombies blindly follow the lead of these celebrities.

Most celebrities are so full of themselves that even the richest and most successful of them aren't content with their kingdoms on the big screen—they have to do commercials, too, taking work away from the rank-and-file Screen Actor's Guild actor who barely makes enough to qualify for union health insurance.

Catherine Zeta-Jones married into Hollywood royalty when she became Michael Douglas's wife, and even if she weren't an Oscar-winning actress (*Chicago*) in her own right, she'd never have to work another day in her life if she so chose.

But no, she has to shill for T-Mobile in television commercials. Come on, Catherine Zeta-Jones. Commercials are beneath you! Other actors appear in commercials overseas.

But for celebrities, it's never enough. It's always "me, me, me." Lindsay Lohan complains about the paparazzi but shows up in places where she knows damn well there will be photographers.

Michael Moore sat next to former president Jimmy Carter at the 2004 Democratic National Convention. And the Democrats wonder why America rejected their candidate!

Even if you agree with what Moore says, you probably don't agree with how he says it, even as he's collecting millions from the liberal zombies on the far left that he panders to.

Ann Coulter is just as bad.

In her 2006 book *Godless,* she takes issue with a group of 9/11 widows who she says are using their celebrity to further a political agenda. Coulter's point is that these women are untouchable due to their "widow" status.

That's all well and good, until she gets personal.

Calling them "harpies" who look like they're enjoying their husbands' deaths, she goes on to say: "And by the way, how do we know their husbands weren't planning to divorce these harpies? Now that their shelf life is dwindling, they'd better hurry up and appear in *Playboy.*"

Now that's just plain mean, isn't it? I think the biggest insult one could give Coulter is that she's now just like Michael Moore.

But celebrities and pundits aren't the only reason why we're all in trouble.

TV news anchors and sports broadcasters are doing their share for the Oblivion cause, and of course athletes and their "look at me" attitude is enough to ruin even the most juvenile games on the planet.

And these sports stars are also paid millions of dollars and it still isn't enough.

They need steroids or endorsements that pay them big bucks, and yet some of our highest paid athletes refuse to sign autographs for fans for fear the fan might make forty bucks on eBay. Give me a break.

Donald Trump isn't content with being a billionaire real estate developer, he also has to write books and do reality television. Kozlowski, Skilling, and Lay at Enron and Tyco weren't satisfied with making huge salaries and getting all the requisite perks that come with being the CEO, they had to go and steal from their companies, and bankrupt their employees in the process.

Newspapers and some news organizations have become so blatant with their political agenda that some of the industry's mighty have fallen (see Dan Rather).

Billy Joel isn't happy with being one of the greatest singer/songwriters in the country, so he feels the need to write a children's book. Ditto Jason Alexander, Jane Seymour, and Madonna. Madonna? Yeah, even the French-kissing exhibitionist has a children's book out there.

Give me a break. Publishers should be ashamed of themselves. I'd take James Frey's "memoir" over Madonna's children's book any day of the week. Despite all of the lies and exaggerations in Frey's *A Million Little Pieces*, it's got to be more honest than any children's book by Madonna.

And speaking of authors, I rolled my eyes along with millions of other baseball fans when the big dunce Jose Canseco wrote a book in which he said the majority of Major League Baseball's stars are on steroids. Little did we know that he was telling the truth.

But on the flip side, if Pete Rose thinks coming clean about gambling in his autobiography should guarantee his acceptance back into baseball and into the Hall of Fame he's sorely mistaken. How convenient for this clown to finally admit to breaking a league rule when he had a book to sell.

From Martha Stewart to Kobe Bryant to the cell phone screamer to the moron who tries to board the elevator before you get off, Oblivions are taking over our great nation. And the fact is, they don't even know it. It's up to us non-Oblivions to call them out on their abhorrent behavior.

Our nation's sanity relies on it.

So without further ado, here is *Grrr! Celebrities Are Ruining Our Country . . . And Other Reasons Why We're All in Trouble.*

Please read it, enjoy it, and pass it on—but most of all, Keep On Grrring!

$$(((\quad 1 \quad)))$$

An Open Letter to
the Oblivion Council

TO: THE OBLIVION COUNCIL
FROM: ASPIRING OBLIVION

To Whom It May Concern:

I am writing the council in the hopes of obtaining my Oblivion pin.

For years now I have played by society's written and unwritten rules. I limited my groceries to only ten items in the express checkout lane, and I even returned my cart to the cart corral in the parking lots of grocery stores everywhere.

But I noticed something missing in my life.

I noticed that there are Oblivions in the world who count forty cans of dog food as one item and still get through the express checkout lane. I noticed these Oblivions leaving their shopping carts wherever they please, allowing them to roll into the automobiles of hard-working Americans.

And I said to myself, "Self, wouldn't that be a great way to live? Wouldn't it be great to be so oblivious to everybody in the world that I only had to worry about myself?"

I could wave my arms indiscriminately with a lit cigarette in my hand, oblivious to the people around me and their petty little arm burns. I can smoke my cigarette or my cigar in a crowded restaurant with complete abandon.

I could walk from blackjack table to blackjack table at Las Vegas casinos playing one hand at each. Heck, I can even split tens if I feel so inclined. It's my money, after all.

I could scream at my kid's soccer coach and the referees if my kid's not playing well, blame their teachers if they have bad grades, and point the finger at MTV when my daughter gets pregnant.

It all sounds like too much fun to pass up.

That's why I'm applying for my Oblivion pin. With it comes advantage. I won't leave home without it.

I now know that handicap parking and the fire lanes are spots reserved just for me. I understand that the lines at Starbucks or the Post Office are for poor schmucks who think that being kind to neighbors will actually get them ahead in life.

What a bunch of baloney.

You know, I like to stop short in the middle of busy sidewalks to use my cell phone. I like to speak loudly into my cell phone no matter where I am, and when I'm bored I like to call my friends, no matter what time of the day or night it is. And I love to change my ring tones frequently, especially during times when there is enough peace and quiet around me so I can really concentrate on choosing the right melody.

I noticed an Oblivion the other day who stepped in front of a long line at the Barnes and Noble bookstore just to "ask a quick question." She wanted to know if the book that she put on hold was behind the counter.

The clerk stopped what he was doing to search for the book. He asked the Oblivion under what name the book was held. The Oblivion gave her name, but alas, there was no book. "Oh wait," the Oblivion said. "I put it under my maiden name. See, I signed up on the Web site before I got married, so I always use my maiden name when I deal with Barnes and Noble. Could you check under Dumbich?"

Sure enough, the clerk found the book under Dumbich. He handed it over the counter.

That's when Ms. Dumbich, the Oblivion, uttered words that convinced me once and for all to apply for membership as an Oblivion.

"Well, since I'm up here," she said, "can you ring me up?"

And he did. And aside from a few audible sighs on the line, nobody said a word. Out of the fifteen or so people whom she rudely cut in front of, not one said a single word in protest!

Ms. Dumbich was obviously sporting her pin.

Therefore, I humbly and with full conviction would like to apply for my Oblivion pin.

I promise to wear it with neglect and never even acknowledge the existence of any higher authority other than myself. I promise to behave like I wear blinders, and I promise to see only what is directly in front of me and only what applies to me.

I will not let the Oblivion Council down. Thank you for your consideration.

Sincerely, I.M. Oblivious
Oblivion-in-Training

$(((\quad 2 \quad)))$

Grrring at the Movies and Other Theater Annoyances

Like Tim Robbins says in the Steven Spielberg remake of *War Of The Worlds*, "They planned this for millions of years."

To paraphrase Paul Revere, "The Oblivions are coming, the Oblivions are coming!"

Oblivions have been around since the dawn of time. Thousands of years ago there were cavemen who annoyed other cavemen without ever knowing it. They grunted nonstop, or they flung the fleas off their bodies onto their fellow cavemen and cavewomen with complete abandon.

Times may have changed, but the Oblivions haven't.

Case in point: Have you been to any good movies lately?

SIT BACK AND RELAX . . . ENJOY THE SHOW

Movie theaters are breeding grounds for Oblivions, and therein lies the Grrr!, because most people love going to the movies. There's nothing better than sitting in a theater when the lights go down and that first preview fills the screen. Our stomachs get butterflies in the hope that we're about to see a cinematic masterpiece.

But notice I said I get butterflies watching *previews*. Commercials make me go Grrr!

When the practice of showing commercials at the movie theater became acceptable is beyond me. It all comes down to consumers having no guts to tell theater owners where to shove their commercials.

Paying $6.00 for a bucket of fifty-cent popcorn and $3.50 for a pack of Twizzlers is one thing. But paying $10.50 for a movie ticket and then being forced to watch a Pepsi or a Fandango commercial should be beyond reason.

Yet we watch in silence.

We Grrrind our teeth, but we keep going back, week after week, lining the pockets of studio bigwigs, theater owners, and morally bankrupt, spoiled, self-centered celebrities.

It's time we all collectively say, "I'm mad as hell, and I'm not going to take it anymore"—with thanks of course, to Paddy Chayefskyi, the writer of *Network*.

Start demanding refunds when the theater owners shove commercials down your throat, because in two more months the movie will be out on DVD anyway, and then you can watch in the privacy of your own home, sans commercials.

But wait. No, that would be too good wouldn't it?

Thanks to the greedy movie moguls, you'll get the commercials at home, too, and to add insult to injury the movie distributors love to send out those DVDs with the fast-forward and skip functions disabled, so that when it comes to their precious commercials and promotions, you're a captive audience.

Hmm. Didn't I just pay $19.99 for this?

You know, the whole commercial thing wouldn't be so bad if Madison Avenue gave two hoots about the quality of the commercials we see at the movies. And since we're in the movie theater, you'd think that maybe you'd see a movie star or two starring in a movie theater commercial, as opposed to the small screen like Zeta-Jones.

Better yet, they should start showing commercials based on the rating of the film you're about to see.

Imagine a condom ad starring Halle Berry and Billy Bob Thornton before a rated-R flick? They can reenact a scene from *Monster's Ball.*

How about an ad for Johnnie Walker Black featuring home video from Nick Nolte's private collection? Joaquin Phoenix can sing his way through a commercial for the complete Johnny Cash CD collection.

John Woo can direct an ad for a sports car featuring *The Transporter's* Jason Statham doing his own stunt driving. Lindsay Lohan can do ads for diet pills and Sean Penn can do them for Smith and Wesson. Ducati sport motorcycles can hire Gary Busey to demonstrate why wearing a helmet while doing 125 mph on a motorcycle is a good idea.

Keanu Reeves can reprise his *Matrix* role as Neo in ads for iPod, downloading music into his brain, while his *Speed* costar Sandra Bullock would be a perfect pitchwoman for Harley Davidson, which she could costar in with her husband, Jesse James of West Coast Choppers fame.

Paris Hilton can do ads for Jenna Jameson movies. At least she'd be in her element and doing what she does best, which I'm still trying to figure out.

At least those commercials would be interesting, right?

Instead, we get some fat schmuck licking an automobile clean with his tongue in an ad for online movie tickets. I don't even get the correlation.

You know, I used to be an actor, and I did several commercials in the hopes that one would give me enough exposure to help me get to the next level in my career. So to an extent, I can understand an actor having to act ridiculous in a spot. But I would never, ever, lick an automobile with my tongue for anything. I don't care how clean they make it, or if they flavor it with some tasty fruit flavoring or even 25-year-old Macallan whiskey.

What do you think the actor's agent told the guy?

"Hey, remember in acting class when they told you to be the tree? Well, just be the sponge. Be the sponge. That's your motivation."

Come on, all you highly paid creative geniuses in the advertising community. Give us something we can really sink our teeth into at the movie theater. What do you have to lose? With TiVo and other DVR technologies becoming ubiquitous in the home, you're going to have to start looking elsewhere to hawk your wares.

Since commercials in movie theaters don't seem to be going anywhere, at least make them watchable.

But let's get back to the Oblivions in the theaters.

Ever notice that movie theaters are perfect for little Oblivions-in-training?

Oblivion parents love to drop their little monsters off at the movies for two and a half hours of unsupervised, sugar-induced dementia, or even worse, they'll drag their kids to movies that *they* want to see, no matter how inappropriate the movie may be for the kids.

"Gee, I don't know why little four-year-old Jenny is crying. The explosions aren't *that* scary."

But listen, these days, at least one can reasonably expect that the kids are going to be rambunctious and/or disrespectful.

Sadly, in the new millennium, that's just the way it is. Parents are too busy playing video games or complaining about how they're not getting ahead at the office, so parenting is the furthest thing from their minds.

So what do you do?

God knows you can't say anything, because then some Oblivion parent will start a fight with you or the Oblivion child will tell you you're "not the boss of me."

So, you figure to go to the movies on a weekday or several weeks *after* a film opens, so that you can avoid the crowds and said Oblivions. That should be a safe play, don't you think?

But Just When You Thought It Was Safe to
Go Back in the Water . . .

So you and your date or your buddies walk into the movie theater, and wouldn't you know it, the whole place is empty. You can't believe your luck.

Now, even though every seat is yours for the taking, you know better than to sit in the middle two seats at the most centered part of the theater, because that's a desirable location, and if anyone does comes in, they're bound to sit in front of you. You know that. So you find a perfect spot just to the right or left of center.

There, perfect. Perfect seat. Perfect view. Perfect access to the aisle. Perfect.

Why, then, does the only other couple to arrive in the theater still decide they want to sit directly in front of you?

It never fails. No matter where you sit, no matter how empty the theater is, they'll pick those two seats right in front of you! Or worse, right behind you, so they can eat and drink and shake the ice in their cups right at ear level.

I don't know about you, but the sound of people munching on food or shaking ice is music to my ears!

These Oblivions munch on their popcorn as if they were dying of some rare disease, and the only cure lies at the bottom of the bucket in the form of one of those hard, unpopped kernels.

It's relentless. *Shoomp*—the hand goes into the bucket. *Shoomp shoomp*—it pulls out a handful of popcorn. *Munch munch munch*—breathe—*munch munch munch*—breathe—and then *shoomp*, in for round two, until there is no more popcorn to scarf.

I once applauded a man in a Manhattan theater when he finished his bag of popcorn. Not only was he munching like a horse, but when he couldn't dive his greasy fingers (loudly I should add) into the bag for any more buttery treasure, he tipped his head back and emptied the crumbs into his mouth. As if that wasn't enough, he then crumpled up the bag and dropped it on the floor.

Unbelievable.

Of course, being an Oblivion, this jackass has no idea how loud, how rude, or how disgusting he was. No idea whatsoever. All he knew was that he was hungry for popcorn.

"I'm at the movie theater and, dammit, I'm going to eat popcorn."

Look, there are millions of popcorn lovers out there and the majority of them at least know how to eat. But it only takes one Oblivion to spoil it for the rest of us. The next time you're at the movies, close your eyes and imagine an army of rats rummaging around in the dark.

The collective sound is so bad that if movie theaters had headphone jacks at every seat and rented noise cancellation headphones at ridiculous prices, I'd pay the extra money just so that my movie experience wasn't rudely brought back to the reality of Oblivionism minutes into the film.

Of course Oblivion kids, seat stalkers, and obnoxious chewers aren't the only dangers at the movie theater. Just as bad are the people who— despite thirty minutes of annoying commercials and previews and petitions for donations to various charities—still manage to show up *after* the movie starts.

After the movie starts!

Not only do these morons disrupt the crucial beginning moments of the film by standing in the middle of the aisle pointing out empty seats throughout the theater, they usually spot two in a row that are not together, so they'll have the audacity to ask other paying patrons:

"Can everybody move over one seat so that we can sit together?"

Umm, no! No way. I'm sorry, but I refuse to move when people impose on me. If you think I'm a jerk, then so be it.

Choosing my seats at the theater is a very delicate and exacting process. It's not my problem if grown-ups don't have the wherewithal or the common sense to arrive on time, especially these days.

I know that sounds contradictory—me Grrring the selfish behavior of Oblivions who mean to minimize my own selfishness, but at least the only person I inconvenienced to satisfy my desires was me.

I planned for traffic. I got my Twizzlers and my Coke long before the movie started, and I arrived long enough before the crowds did so that I can sit exactly where I want to sit. And yes, I even went to the bathroom before the movie started.

Imagine that!

So don't ask me to move. I will fight you if I have to. Wild horses couldn't drag me away.

One man sent his wife in for round two after I told him to forget about it. She said, "Sir, you're being unreasonable. Don't make me get the manager." I said, "Good. While you're at it, tell him you're going to reimburse me for my ticket, too, because you're ruining the movie for me." Other people chimed in, "Count me in, too, sweetheart."

Needless to say, they found two seats together in the front row.

Look, folks, nobody knows better than you your own desires.

Get to the theater on time, and if you want to sit together, get there early. It's opening night at one of the most hyped movies of the year, and you think you're going to sit together if you're late? Come on, people!

And don't forget, you'll still be a couple after the movie starts, so I don't really see the problem with being separated for two hours that you'll be sitting through in silence, anyway.

Since there is never a list of movie theater etiquette posted near the box office, here is one that I think non-Oblivions everywhere would probably agree is reasonable.

Movie Theater Etiquette

1. Arrive at least ten minutes *before* the movie starts.
2. Eat your popcorn with your mouth closed.
3. Do not crinkle any type of wrapper or bag.
4. Do not shake the ice in your cup.
5. If you've already seen the film, *do not* give away any plot twists. In fact, don't talk at all.
6. Shut off your cell phone, or at least put it on vibrate. If you must answer it, leave the theater.
7. Don't sit directly in front of or behind the only other two people in the theater.
8. Dispose of your own trash.
9. Be courteous to the employees. They are people and don't deserve your displaced aggression.
10. Don't ask other patrons to move to a different seat.

Grrr!

It really doesn't matter, however, if this list of movie theater etiquette makes it or not. It's only a matter of time before movies are released for one-time viewing on your cable or satellite system or on the Internet. So the days of enduring Oblivions and overpriced popcorn and rude counter clerks and ticket takers and old theaters where the sound is wanting and the screen is dirty and the seats have springs coming out of them will have all gone the way of the standard analog color television.

As if dealing with everything mentioned above—and then some— isn't enough, sometimes the movie just plain stinks. What recourse do we have?

Has anyone ever tried to get his or her money back after seeing a bad movie? I never have. Why do we simply accept bad films?

I guess it's the same principle as getting a bad meal. If you eat it all hoping it will get better, the restaurant won't take it off your bill. The trick is leaving the movie early. But who wants to wait in that long line again, and then plead their case with some kid who speaks broken English (although he's American) and is not authorized to give you a refund anyway? Then you'll have to wait for the manager to come down, and explain all over again. . . . It's just not worth it.

Did I mention I love going to the movies?

LIVE THEATER

I was on Broadway watching Hugh Jackman in *The Boy from Oz.* In what was one of the musical's more poignant moments (and there were few), someone's cell phone went off.

Now, at this point in our technically driven lives, too many people carry cell phones to find this too surprising. As long as there are cell phones, people will forget to turn them off. This is an unfortunate fact that I think we can all live with occasionally.

But this person, in what could only be an attempt to avoid outing him- or herself as the cell phone Oblivion, let it ring twelve times before it finally went to voice mail. Twelve rings in the middle of a Broadway musical!

Dude or Dudette—just reach down and shut it off. Sure, you'll get a few *tsk-tsk*s and dirty looks in your direction, but it's not you're like going to get arrested. Just shut it off.

And while I'm on the subject of Broadway theaters, it's about time for the Shuberts, Nederlanders, Jujamcyns, and whoever else owns theaters, like Disney, to update those old buildings.

After paying $100 to see some washed-up movie star sing her way through *Fiddler On The Roof*, there should at least be more than two stalls and two urinals in the only two bathrooms in the whole theater.

What, did theatergoers in the old days not need to use the restrooms at the same time? There is only *one* intermission, dammit.

And what is with those seats stacked on top of one another? It's time for some stadium seating on Broadway, because sitting behind some Oblivion with her theater hat on isn't going to cut it, and sitting in my neighbor's lap isn't what I bargained for, either.

Let's go. You producers aren't giving tickets away.

When I was an actor I costarred in the Off-Broadway show *Tony n' Tina's Wedding*. This is the play where the audience interacts with the cast as members of the bride's or the groom's family. Most people who know the show will say, "Isn't that the show where you go from the church to the reception?"

Yes, that's the one.

Attending this play is supposed to be like attending the wedding of some over-the-top, crazy relative, complete with the bride's ex-boyfriend, the best man's drug dealing, the groom's father's stripper girlfriend, and the hypochondriac mother of the bride.

It's really a hoot.

But one of the drawbacks of improvising with the audience is when companies, usually Wall Street brokerage firms, think booking the show would be a good idea for an office Christmas party.

Those were the worst nights of my life as an actor.

Try performing for a room full of twentysomething, coked-up, overpaid, immature Armani-wearing Obliviots who all know one another. And did I mention not a single woman among them?

Yeah, there's a great idea. Let's have Sausage Night at Tony n' Tina's Wedding!

Needless to say, I phoned it in on those nights. Of course, being in New York City, acting the part of a stereotypical New York Italian who thinks he's a gangster in the image of Michael Corleone is a little too close to home for some of the audience members.

There were several nights when we had a table full of "cardboard gangsters"—guys who think they're connected but are really just pretenders looking to impress their girlfriends—who think that by kicking some actor's ass they're going to prove how tough they are.

These guys get caught up in the act. See Lilo Brancato Jr. if you don't know what I'm talking about. That clown had the world handed to him after Robert De Niro plucked him off a beach and made him a star in *A Bronx Tale*. A decade later he was involved in a botched robbery attempt that resulted in the death of a New York City police officer.

Cardboard gangsters watch way too much *Sopranos.*—In Brancato's case, he was even on *The Sopranos*. A real stretch, apparently.

But I digress.

The thing about Oblivions is that they are completely and utterly unaware of their rude behavior. The world revolves around them.

They wear invisible blinders so that the only thing they see is what's directly in front of them—which is usually exactly what they're after. If these people were aware that they were being rude yet continued unabated, they'd simply be jerks. The question is, am I really a jerk because I insist on standing up to the Oblivions? It all depends. Sometimes it's just not worth the effort. Most Oblivions are beyond repair. It all depends on how Grrred I am at the time of the Oblivion's infraction.

Standing up to Oblivions can be rewarding or it can be dangerous. It's up to you to use your best judgment. Here are a few Oblivions I don't recommend you standing up to:

- Real gangsters
- Gomer Pyle–type power-hungry cops
- Wild-eyed panhandlers
- Murderous spouses
- Mike Tyson

MOVIE TRAILERS AND LATE-NIGHT TV

Movie trailers can be pretty annoying, too. Like when the announcer puts on his serious voice and says, "Starring Oscar-nominated [insert name], or Oscar winner [insert name], or from the Oscar-winning director of [insert title]."

Puhleez! We're not that dumb.

If the trailer stinks we're not going to see the movie, no matter how many Oscar nominees or winners are in it (even if mentioning the Oscar is in the stars' contracts). Grrr!

And why aren't there any women doing movie trailer voice-overs? It's always the same tired voice that starts with the same overused line: "In a world where Oblivions have taken over . . ." Sometimes I get chills down my spine just hearing the intense announcer voice. You know the one that gets all sentimental and is meant to tell you how you should be feeling?

It's kind of like watching a Nora Ephron film.

Ever see *You've Got Mail?* There are more songs in that movie to help you, the dumb viewer, understand just how you should be feeling at any particular moment or to help you understand what Tom Hanks or Meg Ryan are going through emotionally as they walk solemnly or skip happily across the screen.

REVERB

Then there are those radio stations whose DJs use the reverb effect. Do DJs think we're out there thinking, "Gee, I wish my voice *echoed* so I could be a radio announcer, too?"

Nobody talks like that!

I wish DJs would just shut the hell up anyway. Can you say thank goodness for satellite radio (although it's not free)? Now, there are of course exceptions to every rule, but for the most part DJs are obnoxious. That's why I love my satellite radio. No commercials and no DJs if I don't want any.

"HE COULD . . . GO . . . ALL . . . THE . . . WAY"

Speaking of "Nobody talks like that," what is it with sportscasters, anyway? Do you think they go home and speak with their significant others in that sports announcer voice? Ever hear Ron "Jaws" Jaworski on ESPN? Funny, when he's in the studio he sounds like a normal guy. But when he's reporting from the field, all of a sudden he sounds like Suzy Kolber. I don't get it. (Hey, Jaws, next time you're on the sideline, better watch out for Joe Namath.)

Chris Boomer sounds like an idiot. And don't even get me going on Stuart "Spoken Word" Scott. These ESPN guys are all hoping they'll be the next Craig Kilborn and get a late-night talk show that nobody watched anyway.

One day I heard my local sportscaster refer to a hockey goal as "right where Mama puts the peanut butter." Huh? But here's the real Grrr! part. Not only did he say it in the 5:30 A.M. hour, he said it again at 6:30 A.M., just in case any new viewers missed his earlier brilliance. Is there a producer in the house? And no, the segment was not recorded. He was live both times.

Of course, hockey fans would know that the sportscaster was referring to a goal that is high up in the net, or "the top shelf." Ohhhh, thanks, Mr. Sportscaster. I'm soooo impressed on how inside you've brought me with your peanut butter analogy. However, most people put the cookies on the top shelf, not the peanut butter. Moron.

REALITY TV CONTESTANTS

And then we have those reality show contestants who move on to bigger and better things in the TV business. Since when did eating bugs on *Survivor* or *Fear Factor* become a prerequisite to having one's own show? I'm going to fire my agent and just eat worms in my next TV piece. I'll be the next host of *American Idol*. Grrr!

SET UP THE CLIP FOR US

Okay. Why are singers asked to sing but actors are never asked to act?

You ever notice that when an actor is a guest on a late-night television show like Leno or Letterman, she gets to sit down on the couch and be interviewed? But when a musician or a rock group is invited on the show, they just get to sing like they are some kind of hired help.

Are actors and their opinions somehow more important than musicians?

Imagine if there were no more movie clips on that monitor that pops up from behind the couch. Instead Naomi Watts, for instance, acts out a scene from *21 Grams* right there on stage. Or Keanu Reeves demonstrates some of the martial arts he mastered while filming *The Matrix*.

Yeah, that'll happen.

Tom Cruise can marvel us with a monologue from the next John Grisham book-turned-film. Drew Barrymore can do a little Shakespeare and Jim Carrey can do some facial contortions.

What's the difference?

Actors are as much performers as musicians are, right? You know what's particularly Grrring about an actor who sits on the couch? When

David Letterman tells him to set up the clip, and the actor pretends he doesn't know which clip they're about to play, like he hasn't watched himself over a million times by now.

Or, how about when the clip is chock-full of action sequences that we all know damn well show stunt doubles doing all the work. I just hate it when the audience claps wildly for a clip filled with explosions, stunts, and special effects. Just who are they clapping for? The stunt co-ordinator isn't up there on the couch. The pyrotechnics engineer is nowhere to be seen. The editor and the special effects animator aren't around, either. He's called an actor for a reason folks. He's playing make-believe and making millions of dollars doing it.

The little people behind the scenes aren't making millions, and they're not getting any applause, either.

THIRTY SECONDS OF HELL

I hate it when television and radio commercials are five decibels *louder* than the program you're watching. You know those nights when you've got insomnia, so you put on some late-late-night talk show that is guaranteed to put you to sleep . . . like Carson Daly . . . and just when you're dozing off the Flowbee commercial blares and just about gives you a heart attack.

But speaking of commercials, am I the only one insulted by celebrity endorsements on TV?

Ryan Seacrest hosts the most popular show on TV and he does wireless commercials that run *during* that show. It's bad enough reality TV is already cutting into the number of jobs available for struggling actors—now their hosts are hogging the commercials, too.

I don't mean to single out Mr. Seacrest. He's obviously worked very hard to get where he is, and he's not on the same level yet—at least financially—as Zeta-Jones or, say, Jason Alexander after *Seinfeld*.

Yet that didn't stop that little roly-poly actor from giving TV viewers agita in the form of KFC commercials. Thank goodness the Colonel cut the head off that ad campaign. At least Jerry Seinfeld's American Express commercials were funny, which made up for the fact that he was already extremely wealthy when he was doing them.

But it's not only actors with the greedy agents—eh, um, with the extra cash opportunities. Sports stars are raking in big bucks from their teams, but many of them will sign only a certain brand of ball or wear only a certain brand of shoe—because they're being paid more big bucks to do so. And we eat it up.

Tiger Woods crossed picket lines and starred in Buick commercials when the Screen Actors Guild was on strike during collective bargaining over commercial fees and the like. Anybody else would have gotten banned from SAG and probably from more commercials and movies. But not Woods. It's all very Grrring and hypocritical. The guy who needs the job is too afraid to do a nonunion commercial that absolutely nobody is going to see because he may lose his SAG card, but multimillionaire Woods does it and he is barely punished. (He reportedly paid a $100,000 fine to the Guild—peanuts to him).

Forget Fido. TiVo is man's best friend.

WEATHER FORECASTERS

Weathercasters must have it rough. I mean, if I'm wrong over fifty percent of the time I think after a while my boss might fire me, but in the case of weathercasters, it's never an issue.

But hey, they're busy being witty, right?

I can imagine it must be tough to come up with witticisms for snow or ice or extreme heat, but I want to scream every time I hear something like, "We're getting more of the white stuff heading our way," or "Ol' Man Winter is making a comeback." Dude, he never left.

BAD TELEPROMPTER READERS

Trust me, it's not as easy as it looks. Reading the teleprompter well takes a lot of practice. But that's why anchors and reporters and hosts get paid good money. Now, not everybody has to be Fox News Channel's Shepard Smith (who is probably the best off-the-top-of-his-head anchor in the business), but there's nothing worse than watching someone on TV bantering with their coanchor in a very natural way, and then all of a sudden sound like a robot when they return to the prompter:

"Up . . . next . . . we'll . . . have . . . an . . . ex-clu-sive . . . interview . . . with . . . so . . . and . . . so." Grrr!

MORNING TELEVISION AND CELEBRITY CHEFS

Ever notice that when morning news shows do budget cooking segments—where chefs show how to make great dishes with inexpensive ingredients—they always use celebrity chefs who own restaurants where the appetizers cost more than the dinner they've created for the segment? Who are they kidding?

ANNOYING PHRASES

In the eighties it was "Word." In the nineties everybody was saying, "Show me the money," after the movie *Jerry Maguire* came out. These days, "It's all good" and "bling, bling" are way-overused phrases. But how about the people who pause each sentence with "but, um-mmm"? I always add "bump" when they do that. "But-um-bump!" That's annoying "as all get out." Another Grrr! phrase.

It doesn't help when news personalities use these stupid phrases to try to show just how hip they are. Yeah, that's what I want to see, some whitebread reporter saying "Bling" to Terrell Owens 'cause, you know, he wants to be as cool as Owens is. Please.

KA-KA-KA-CLASSIC ROCK

I love classic rock music.

Neil Young, the Allman Brothers, the Band, Elton John, the Beatles, Jethro Tull and Aerosmith, among many others, honor my CD library and flow through my car stereo.

But why do so many classic rock radio stations overplay the classics to the point where they're not classics anymore? If I hear "Touch Me" by The Doors one more time I'll, I'll . . . well, I don't know. But it's as if playing Jim Morrison over and over again is a DJ's idea of postgraduate degree work. "Well, professor, when in doubt, play Jim Morrison. It will display your keen insight and in-depth knowledge of the classic rock genre." Yeah, right. Besides, these days DJ's don't even get to play their own music.

And then there's the promo announcer, embellishing the overplayed "classic" as if it were something new; "WWWW! The only place you'll hear," and then abruptly, "Come on, come on, come on now touch me baby—*bah-dump-ba-daaaah*—Can't you see, that I am not afraid."

As if that weren't enough to make your skin crawl, the promo producer will obnoxiously produce the station identification sounder, so that it sounds something like (in a deep, powerful voice): "From the top of the highest tower in some city—WWWW . . . Ka-Ka-Ka-Ka-Ka-Classic Rock!"

Hey, we listen to classic rock because we don't buy into the hype! Grrr!

When I was in college I was a DJ at a fifties-themed bar called Wurlitzer's. Every night the same people would come up to me and request the same songs, over and over again. If I never hear "Brown Eyed Girl" again I will die a happy man. What boggled my mind was after the hundredth time hearing the same song these people would still act all goofy and run to the dance floor as if they were hearing it for the first time.

There are so many clichéd tunes that simply drive me up the wall. If I go to a bar and the soundtrack is full of songs like "Paradise by the Dashboard Light" and "Working for the Weekend," I know I'm in the wrong place.

They're probably selling "shooters," too. Woohoo! Yeah, that's what I want: some sugary-tasting syrup that could double as Robitussin from someone's minibeaker. What's next, a throat culture to Warren Zevon's "Werewolves In London"?

The Critics: Taking Movies Way Too Seriously

You ever wonder if film critics tire of movie companies clipping quotes from their reviews?

Especially from Thanksgiving through New Year's Day, when Hollywood pushes its year-end movie blitz (another Grrr! because movie lovers are forced to squeeze in all the best movies in one month right before Oscar nominations), oft-quoted critics might see their credibility become marginalized when several movie ads appear side-by-side in newspapers.

In scanning the *St. Louis Post-Dispatch* one Thanksgiving, looking for a movie to go see, I came across several quotes from the same famous critic over two pages of film ads. To be fair, movie studios can clip quotes from film reviews without the critic's knowledge or even his consent. But here they are from the paper anyway:

On *Alexander*: "[Colin Farrell] turns up the heat as Alexander. . . . The film lives up to its size."

On *Sideways*: "You won't have a better time at the movies this year."

On *The Incredibles*: "It's James Bond, Indiana Jones, and the X-Men all rolled into one kick-out-the-jams spectacle. . . . One of the year's best."

On *Kinsey*: "Kinsey wanted to snap the public out of sexual ignorance. And Condon's knockout of a movie tries to do the same. You'll be shocked at how far we haven't come."

On *Ray*: "Electrifying. . . . [Jamie] Foxx's fierce, funny, deeply felt performance deserves to be legendary."

All of these quotes are from one film critic, Peter Travers of *Rolling Stone* magazine. Now, I like reading Travers's reviews. I think he's pretty honest and knowledgeable about the movie business, but I can't help but think that even he would cringe when presented with two pages of ads quoting from his film reviews.

The number of those appearances diminishes his credibility, whether he likes it or not. Indeed, whether my statement is true or not—readers will begin to wonder if there is any movie that Mr. Travers doesn't like.

But let's look more closely at the quotes.

"The film lives up to its size." Well, that hardly encourages me to rush out and see *Alexander*. Maybe he saw it in IMAX? I don't know.

"You won't have a better time at the movies this year." Well, I suppose if you happen to go see *Sideways* when you're in a really, really good mood, or on a first date with the man or woman of your dreams, perhaps that statement is true, otherwise that's a pretty big assumption.

"Rolled into one kick-out-the-jams spectacle." I'm still trying to figure out what that even means. Are we supposed to go in our pajamas? Is it a martial arts reference? Is Michael Jordan in it?

"Kinsey wanted to snap the public out of sexual ignorance." Hmmm. After hundreds of years of procreation, I somehow don't buy that argument. Besides, today Kinsey might be labeled a pervert. It kind of reminds me of when I comment to Mrs. Grrr about how that (gorgeous) woman over there would leave the house wearing that short skirt, stockings and thigh-high boots—*tsk*ing all the way even as I smash headfirst into the parking meter. Bam!

I don't mean to pick on Travers. If you want to see his full reviews, visit *Rolling Stone* on the Web or buy the magazine. The point is, the movie companies aren't fooling any of us. If the movie's good, we'll take our friend's word for it way before any blurb.

Less Is More:
The "Overproduced"
Man and Woman

When is enough enough? Everyday we see men and women with too much stuff on. Too much cologne, too much perfume, too much makeup, too many accessories—the list goes on and on.

Young girls are walking through the malls dressed like prosti-tots, wearing tank tops with no bras and sweatpants going up their behinds with the word JUICY stitched across their young posteriors.

In TV we call it *Overproduced.*

Ever see a television program that is so full of whizbang effects that the viewer becomes distracted from the content?

These shows mix black-and-white and color video, are filled with music pops, jump cuts, flying graphics, and wacky shot transitions. What it usually means is the producer is either short on talent or short on content and these effects jazz up an otherwise boring program.

But TV isn't the Grrr! here.

It's the Overproduced man or woman.

Remember the Real-ities on the A&E program *Growing Up Gotti*? The three young Gotti boys, who are Victoria Gotti's sons, were so Overproduced it was difficult to watch the show.

Their eyebrows were waxed Bette Davis–thin, their hair was gelled and blow-dried so much these guys looked like they were going up for the role of Heat Miser in the school play ("What ever I touch starts to melt in my clutch—I'm too much").

Plus the Gotti boys had that overall "I don't care how I look, but it takes an hour of careful caring to get it right" wardrobe feel. Just who were these guys catering to, the Village People?

But the Gottis aren't the only guys waxing, plucking, and grooming themselves within an inch of their lives. Go to any Gold's Gym on the East Coast and you'll see a bunch of muscle-bound guys who look like they spent too much time in front of their older sister's vanity. I'm not sure when the overgrooming of hairy men started, but please stop it.

A little plucking between the eyebrows is quite all right, if not completely necessary, so as to avoid the Neanderthal look we all had in our eighth-grade class picture. But it's gone way too far.

However women are the more frequently Overproduced.

Here's a good example. On a bus one day I saw a very beautiful woman who could have used a little style editing.

She wore two toe rings on each of her tanned, silver-nail-polished feet, white sandals, and a white coral ankle bracelet. She had on three earrings—one on the inside of her ear—a pink miniskirt manufactured to look like she had cut it herself with a pair of scissors, a navel ring, a flower tattoo on the small of her back, and more makeup than I could record in my one fleeting glance. (What? I'm not a stalker or anything—insert evil laugh here.)

But here's the real Grrring part: She used the bus as her own vanity and put on at least three different colors of mascara. First there was the standard black, like most women wear. Then she put on a white highlight to the edges of her lashes, and then she pulled out another brown brush to mesh it all together with.

She did the same to her lips using two colors, gloss, and then a pencil to outline that perfect lip shape. She then applied more makeup and powder to her cheeks. Her makeup bag looked like a blood-filled tick, and from the way she was going at her face with the powder I figure she'll have severe arthritis in her wrists, or at the very least, carpal tunnel syndrome, by the time she's twenty-four.

When this woman got off the bus she looked like something out of a Britney Spears video. The point is, she was beautiful before all the stuff. By the time she was finished, she looked well, Overproduced.

But while I'm on the subject ladies, . . . if you dress for attention, you're going to get it. If you're not wearing a bra at the office and your high beams are on, don't get upset when guys look at you. When you're wearing high heel pumps and stockings with the seam going up the back so that our eyes trace the line up to your miniskirt, and you catch us looking, don't get upset at us about it.

If you build it, we will, errr, well, you know the rest.

PROSTI-TOTS AND MILFS IN TRAINING

The prosti-tot phenomenon is an example of how Hollywood mores, or lack thereof, continue to negatively influence our nation.

Remember when the Olsen twins turned eighteen? There was such fascination with the child stars that it became an obsession on the Internet and on various late night comedy and even sports programming, that there were countdowns to their birthday seemingly everywhere you looked.

These countdowns were there so that the men who fantasized about the prepubescent looking teens didn't feel like complete pervs.

The same countdown occurred when Long Island temptress Lindsay Lohan turned legal.

It's disgusting, and a direct result of how the people who run our entertainment industry target children with advertising and programming and encourage them to grow up into objects of desire. It all adds up to the loss of innocence.

There's so much talk about how violence in movies and in video games can lead to violent children, some even going so far as to blaming the video game *Doom* for the Columbine School shooting. But nobody is pointing their finger at the Disney Channel because Hillary Duff is wearing tight jeans and halter tops, are they?

No, parents are buying tight jeans and halter tops for their teenage girls.

PLASTIC SURGERY

Which brings us to that other phenomenon we can also blame celebrities for: the ubiquity and mainstream acceptance of plastic surgery.

There was once a time when plastic surgery was only talked about in shameful whispers at country club luncheons.

"Did you see Joan's nose? Funny how she goes away on holiday for two weeks and returns with a little pixie nose." Nowadays Joan and people like her are celebrated among friends for "doing something for herself."

Good for her.

When I was in Hollywood covering the 2006 Academy Awards I ran into two ex-girlfriends who are now actresses of some success. I hadn't seen either of these women in more than ten years, and the thing that struck me about them is that they had breasts.

Big breasts.

Being a small guy, I've never been attracted to women with huge busts; in fact, most women I'm attracted to are petite. I was beginning to wonder what I saw in these girls when I was younger, but then it dawned on me. Implants.

Now, plastic surgery can be a terrific thing for a lot of people. A little adjustment on the nose can go a long way in making one feel that much better about oneself, and some added firmness to the breast can be just what the doctor ordered, especially for women who've had children and are looking to get them perky again.

But for those plastic surgery addicts who get Botoxed, face-lifted, nipped, tucked, and sucked year after year, the whole practice is not only dangerous to their health, it's also ugly.

Joan Rivers looks like she's been vacuum sealed, and her eyes don't seem to be in the same spot God put them. Watching *Dr. 90210* on E! is enough to make most people terrified to travel west.

Indeed, during all my time in Hollywood I wondered how any normal-looking person can ever make it in the movies. Everybody out there is thin as a rail, and diet obsessed, or more accurate, they want everybody to think they are diet obsessed.

"Can I have the Cobb salad with the low fat dressing, on the side, and water with lemon?" When the Cobb comes and, gasp, there's so much meat on it . . . "Didn't I order the garden salad?"

Lest anyone they know walk by their table and witness such diet indiscretions!

They have trainers, dieticians, wardrobe stylists, hair stylists, facial technicians who use lasers to remove unwanted facial hair at a thousand bucks a clip, and manicures and pedicures that start at a hundred bucks.

Who are these people?

They live in tiny houses or apartments but lease Mercedes that probably cost more than their mortgages. They have five hundred-square-feet dwellings but state-of-the-art plasma televisions hanging on their walls with the twenty-thousand-dollar surround sound system.

They're bartenders and waiters living hand-to-mouth but won't think twice about buying a pair of $200 Lucky Brand jeans just because they're in. And they'll wear those jeans every day.

Perception is everything in Hollywood, and the majority of people are commitment-phobic. Nobody wants a significant other because somebody better (looking) might be waiting right around the corner. Nobody wants to sign with an agent as much as "freelance" with an agent, because as soon as any agent gets them the big gig they're going to sign with a bigger agency—because that's the thing to do.

And forget about getting a well-paying acting job on television.

Network Exec: "Well, Trent Zack [all actors think they need two first names], we are prepared to offer you a starring role in our next big television series. What do you say?"

Trent Zack: "I don't know Mr. Exec, I might be reading for Scorsese sometime in the next decade, and I don't want to be typecast as a TV actor. I'd much rather wait on tables or serve beers to you at Skybar."

Trent Zack then spends two hours fussing with his shirt and his hair to get that just-out-of-bed look. Why not just get out of bed? He's also busy ordering Mojitos when he goes out because when in Rome . . .

If anyone reading this wants to be a star, just go to Hollywood. You'll be a star, all right. You'll be an overnight sensation . . . at Skybar.

But sadly, these are the people who, once they make it, become pop culture influences. People who could barely wait on tables are suddenly asked their opinion on politics. People who can't maintain a relationship are asked what they look for in a mate. People who couldn't catch a lob are asked who they're rooting for in the big game and what fabrics do they like for their underwear.

Suddenly women who never had children before know which stroller is the best on the market.

These celebrities are influencing thousands of people across the country, even moving markets. Why? For no other reason than to keep our collective attention.

Members of the media need something to talk about, and since most media outlets are also owned by the same companies that employ celebrities and count on those celebrities to drive ratings and box office sales, suddenly Matt Lauer is interviewing the stars of *Law and Order* on *Today*, and former *Survivor* contestants "Boston Rob" Mariano is a contributing correspondent on CBS News' *The Early Show*, and Jenna Morasca a frequent guest.

Huh?

Here's a news flash for all celebrities and celebrity makers. America is getting smarter, and pretty soon we'll actually prefer our pop stars to be able to sing. We might expect our movie stars to be able to act, not just look good, and we certainly don't want our newscasters doubling as shills for shows we're not interested in watching in the first place.

MEN BEHAVING BADLY

We were all young once, weren't we?

We've all made mistakes in the dating department, right?

Of course we have.

Both men and women make their fair share of poor decisions, and I'm no exception. I didn't really start dating a variety of women until after college. In high school I was a one-woman guy, and I had my heart broken so bad that it took me nearly four years to even begin dating again.

So one could say that I was late entering the dating game, and my immaturity in my early twenties, living in New York City, working the overnights at CBS News and acting in a play called *Tony n' Tina's Wedding*, I was thrown into the fire, so to speak, when it came to dating.

Most of the women I met were audience members at my Off-Broadway play, where I costarred as little Johnny Nunzio, the brother of the groom. As I mentioned earlier, *Tony n' Tina's* is an interactive play, where audience members are actually part of the show, and one of Johnny's character traits was that he would hit on any woman his height.

Each night the men of the cast had a ritual, where we would spy out the dressing room door and watch for the hottest group of women to leave the theater. Then we'd count to about twenty, and descend the back stairs of the theater so that we'd emerge from the stage door at exactly the same time the tomatoes, as we called them, emerged from the theater.

An Open Message To Mrs. Grrr!

Dear Mrs. Grrr! (and all the other wives, girlfriends, husbands, and boyfriends out there who like to ask *benign questions* of their significant others) . . .

While we're flattered that you think we are the smartest people in the world, allow me to get some things off our chests.

o I don't know what the guy in front of us thinks he's doing when he suddenly cuts over to the left lane without signaling.

o I really don't know what's going on over there where two police officers have that car pulled over, and I don't know why the kid in the little Honda Civic has a huge spoiler on the back, other than that he's an idiot.

o I don't know when the city is going to fix that pothole or when the empty lot on the corner will have its lawn mowed.

o When I get up from my chair in the living room, I'm probably going to the bathroom, getting a beer, or am just stretching. I live here. Do I have to answer to "Where are you going" every time I move?

o I didn't make up the rules of society. When I go to work, saying, "*Okay, byeee,*" like I'm leaving you to go to some party is not a good way for me to start my day.

Grrr!

Continued

o I don't know why the music in Chili's is so loud that people can't hold a conversation, but if it bothers you that much, let's leave.

o When the counter clerk at the retail store is nasty I don't know what to think her problem is.

o I'm not sure why the high occupancy vehicle lanes are marked with diamonds, other than that's just what the DMV decided.

o I don't know when the neighbors will have that giant stump on their front lawn removed.

o That's what accountants are for.

Grrr!

The ladies always got a kick out of the fact that I didn't actually "tawlk like dis" in real life, and somehow that made me an "ac-toor," somewhere on par with Lawrence Olivier in their untrained eyes.

I wasn't going to argue.

While my character had a knack of always finding the best-looking woman in the audience to interact with—well, the best-looking single woman in the audience, that is—little "Johnny Boy" gained a reputation as one of the cast studs.

Notice I said, "in the audience." More on that later.

In real life, however, I was nowhere near as entertaining as my character; and believe me, it takes a lot of energy to put on seven shows a week. Imagine going to your brother's wedding six days a week, twice on Saturdays and twice on Sundays. And oh, did I mention I was working the overnights, 1 A.M. to 9 A.M. on the news desk at CBS Radio Sunday through Thursday? Not to mention auditions, acting classes, and the various commercials and small parts here and there?

Needless to say, my time and energy was limited, and trying to fit in the social life of an Off-Broadway star was taxing, to say the least (and I use the term *star* loosely). The fact that I was trying to be a serious actor didn't help my real-life persona, because back then I thought that meant always wearing a black turtle neck and carrying on with my head down and a serious look on my face, reading Uta Hagen, Stanislavski, and Shakespeare on the subway.

Needless to say, some of the tomatoes who dated me after the show were more interested in Johnny than Mike, so I was not nearly as successful as one might imagine. But I did have my share of second dates, and it was here where I fell way short as a man—in the breaking-up department, that is.

I hope you don't hold what I'm about to say too much against me.

I was not a good breaker-upper.

Come on, guys. You know the deal, right? I had this convoluted notion that if I did not make any promises of everlasting love, or if I did not hook up with these women, and if I didn't think there was any chance for a relationship, that I could simply fall off the face of the earth.

In other words, I stopped calling, answering my phone, or returning messages.

One clever girl who I was trying to blow off after a few dates left a message posing as a casting director. I called back as soon as I retrieved the message only to discover that the role I would be reading for was that of the "oh-so-busy guy who didn't have time for a relationship and blah, blah, blah—you got me good."

She called me an asshole and hung up.

Another time I went to meet a girl at a restaurant—and here's where the best-looking girl "in the audience" came into play. I walked into Carmine's restaurant looking for the beautiful tomato whom I met at Saturday night's show, but she was nowhere to be seen.

Actually, I looked right past her. When she approached me I didn't recognize her at all, and she was not even my type. I couldn't imagine what I was thinking. Then it hit me. Saturday night's show was booked by an entire group of real estate agents, and she was the cutest of the bunch. She was not cute anymore.

I made up some excuse about having a rehearsal and got a raincheck. Never mind that the girl came all the way into the city from Queens. What a jerk I was.

Another time I set up a date to meet a woman at a restaurant before my show. I told her I had to be at the theater for a 6:45 P.M. call time, and that we'd meet at 5 P.M. for dinner at Fiorello's, a great Italian restaurant by Lincoln Center.

I stood outside for about forty minutes.

Now, I wasn't too upset about this. After all, it's New York City, and about a million things can happen that could cause travel delays. It wasn't until she arrived that I got upset.

"Why so late?" I asked, fully expecting something about traffic or subway trauma. What I got basically set off my Grrr side.

"I'm the woman," she said. "It's my prerogative to be late."

With that I turned and walked away, never to see or hear from her again. I may have overreacted. After all, she was probably kidding.

There are also many memories of the times I simply stopped calling that make me cringe.

I can recall two times that I was too much of a coward to properly break up with someone. At these times I *know* I was wrong, and if by chance any of those women happen to be reading, I truly apologize. I have no excuse for such ignorant behavior.

One girl freaked me out by putting her makeup on in front of me. When I asked her why she didn't just go use the bathroom, she said she didn't want to leave my side. I panicked and never called her again.

Another woman used to laugh hysterically at my first draft of a one-man show I did in an Off-Broadway theater called *Mat Rat*, which was about my times as a wrestler and martial artist.

Remember, I was being very serious and dramatic back then, and I figured anybody who thought that my stuff was that good the first time out was suspect. I dumped her without any explanation.

Mind you, both of these women—the makeup girl and the laughing girl—were simply being nice to me. They might have actually loved me, and I wasn't ready to be loved. Instead of coming to terms with that self-awareness, I convinced myself that there was something wrong with *them*.

Both were stunningly beautiful people, inside and out, and ultimately it would be my loss.

"YOU TALKIN' TO *ME*?"

Near the beach on the Jersey Shore there's an Italian deli that takes its food very seriously. The cold cuts are the best money can buy, the refrigerator is filled with homemade pastas and other Italian specialties and they take pride in their freshly filled cannoli.

The owners are transplanted Italian-American New Yawkers who are probably the nicest store owners you'll ever meet, who take time to prepare your order just the way you like it, only better, and the men and women behind the counter call everyone "doll," "honey," and "sweetie."

Nothing Grrring there, except when the various clientele decide they want to play a role, and the fake Italians, or "the Sopranos," as I like to call them, come out.

These people may very well be Italian-Americans (or at least look Italian), but they're mostly third and fourth generation nowadays. And they think when pronouncing any food of Italian origin, they need to drop the final vowel, and that somehow ingratiates them to the owners of the Italian specialty deli.

You ever notice these folks?

Mozzarella cheese becomes *Mozzarell*, but it's pronounced "moots-a-rell," and all of a sudden they're speaking so loudly in a newly formed baritone they may as well call it "moots-a-yell."

Prosciutto di Parma becomes "pra-shoot-dee-parm," and "at $24.99 a pound, it better be da best pra-shoot you ever seen."

Manicotti is "mani-got"—not sure where the G comes from there. *Escarole* loses its front E, so it's "scarrrrole"—make sure to roll the Rs. And *gnocchi* is "neeyawk," naturally.

Antipasto? You got it, "anti-Past"—don't forget to pop the P.

I even heard one customer order an Italian combo hoagie but "no toe-mott." I assumed, as did the counter help, the woman meant no tomatoes, but when did tomatoes become Italian?

And don't even think about ordering a tray of meatballs without qualifying them. "I'll take a tray-a-meatballs . . . niccccccce"—as if without the nice the owners would serve a "tray of meatballs . . . grosssssss."

What amazes me more about these Sopranos is that once they leave the confines of the Italian specialty deli, they become Americans again. They lose the swagger and the accent and they're also inconsistent with the dropping of the last vowel.

Why isn't *pepperoni pizza* pronounced "pepperone peets"? I don't get it.

Do you think they went to the movies to see Meryl Streep in The Devil Wears Prad, instead of *The Devil Wears Prada*, or The Da Vince Code?

Do you think their dream car is a "Maser-at"? Of course not, it's most definitely a Maserati, and the speed bike Ducati is not a Doo-Cot.

Is Supreme Court Justice Antonin Scalia "Anton Sca-Lee"? How about Ol' Blue Eyes? I've never heard any Italian call him "Frank Si-Not"!

"Robert De Neer," "Al Pacheen," "Andrea Bochell," "Luciano Pava-Rott," "Camille Pag," "Isabella Rosselleen," "Michaelange," "Leonard Da Vince."

We can go on and on like this.

While many Italian-Americans have picked up this way of speaking from their parents and grandparents, I suspect many of them just watch way too much television.

Oh, well, I guess I'll just order my manicotti with a side of meatballs without the extra flair, and hope when I get home, it'll be just as nice as the dish served to the guy who ordered "mani-got with a side-a meat-a-balls . . . nicccccccce."

Of course, I offended some people with that sentiment after I wrote a GRRR! column on the subject. You know, it wouldn't be America if somebody weren't offended. In this case, it was all of those Sopranos wannabes who become Old Country Italians when they're around foods that end in vowels.

Give me a break.

Besides, I was going for the wannabes, not the real deals. I didn't write the GRRR! as an attack on traditional Italian-American values, as much as I'm not attacking Latin Americans when I say that reporters who take advantage of their Spanish last names by pronouncing them with flair are just as silly as the folks who order their "prra-shoot with melon" appetizer in a loud, boisterous tone.

Like actress Catherine Bell did in the Jim Carrey flick *Bruce Almighty*, when her news anchor character introduces herself as Susan (American accent) Ortega ("Orrrr-Tay-Ga" in a Spanish accent)—several news personalities do the same. They can be reporting in a perfectly Americanized English accent and all of a sudden, when they come to a word of Spanish origin, they dive into the accent.

In New Jersey there's a town called Bogota. It's pronounced "Boh-go-duh," but I once heard a reporter sign off, "In Bogotá, I'm Joe Blow, Something News." Joe Blow is not his real name, but I see this guy on stories every once in a while, so I'm not going to out him here! Anyway, he pronounced it "Bo-goh-TAH." I think I saw the camera shake as the cameraman strained to hold in his laughter.

For a minute I thought I was watching a story about the Medellin drug cartel, and not a flooded basement.

Oops, there I go again. I just offended everybody from Colombia by associating their country with drug rings. I probably offended female camera operators too because I used the term *cameraman*.

The point is, I can offend anyone at anytime by saying practically anything.

Try this:

Of all you Italian-Americans who e-mailed me, not one of you ever rolled your eyes when you heard someone overpronouncing "moots-a-rell"? Come on. Surely watching a weekly show on HBO in which Italian-Americans are portrayed as stupid, bigoted, murdering mobsters is more Grrring than reading about "moots-a-rell," isn't it?

Apparently not.

One offended guy who e-mailed me wrote: "It's like listening to someone pronounce every letter in *hors d'oeuvres*. It's just not right. So, rather than making assumptions and labeling a entire group of people "fake Italians," maybe you should just sit back, have some nice "mani-gat," enjoy the diversity around you and fuggetaboudit."

But don't only stereotypical "fake Italians" say "fuggetaboudit?"

Another guy wrote and said: "Maybe you don't understand how it is to grow up learning this and adopting it. But I for one am proud of it and look forward to teaching my kids our traditions. Even if this tradition doesn't come from Italy, it comes from Italian-Americans."

OK. So you're completely on board with Ebonics, then?

I'm sure every Italian-American named Anthony who screams "moots-a-rell" at the top of his lungs is just peachy when an African-American person calls him "An-Fernee" or "axes him a question."

After all, in many cases, that's how African-Americans are brought up hearing it.

Ooops. There I go again. Great. I've just managed to offend Italian-Americans, Colombian-Americans, and African-Americans in just the last few pages. I'll save you all the hate mail and just print my favorite response, which came from someone who apparently does have a sense of humor. It read simply:

"Uppa U Ace, Straka."

Sounds a lot like my wife.

5

Grrr! Goes Shopping: Mall Is Hell

Malls are chock-full of Oblivions, even more so than movie theaters. Just walking through a mall and observing people can make you want to jump off the second floor balcony and do a belly flop into the center of the food court.

Trying to get any shopping done is like traversing an Oblivion obstacle course.

THE PARKING LOT

People in parking lots crack me up.

The spot stalkers are great. They're the people who will follow you in their cars as you walk to yours, and then sit there with their turn signal on as you load your bags, your kids, and yourself in the car. And then they wave thanks to you as you back out and pull away.

Dude, I was leaving anyway. I didn't leave because I knew you were looking for a spot about ten feet closer to the entrance than the next available spot.

For me, finding a spot is usually very simple. I park far away. Not because I have a nice car. Not because I want to avoid the rogue shopping carts that blow into cars. But because I know that no matter how far away I park, I'm going to walk even farther once I get inside the mall.

What's the use of saving the extra steps outside?

Of course if there weren't a dozen reserved parking spots at every entrance, either for handicapped parking that are seemingly always empty or for curbside pickup for the mall restaurants, there might just be enough spots for everybody.

That's not to say there aren't people who legitimately could use handicapped spots. But there's nothing more Grrring than seeing some clown with a handicapped placard hanging from his rearview mirror, and he's as healthy as any twenty-one-year-old who just won the Boston Marathon.

And don't tell me I'm full of it. We've all seen this guy, and we all envy his resourcefulness at the Department of Motor Vehicles. Don't deny it.

THE ENTRANCE

Once you find your parking spot and trek to the entrance, there always seems to be a line waiting to go through *one door!*

You ever notice that?

There can be a parade of people streaming out and a group of people going in who will wait for everybody to exit before they enter. The Grrr! here is, there's usually three other doors in the lobby that are perfectly functional, but nobody thinks to open them.

Everybody plays follow the leader.

There's something in us that fully accepts the notion that if there is a line, there's got to be a good reason for it. The other doors must be locked, right? Well, not exactly. Go try the door where it's all clear to enter. No strollers coming out. Nobody taking his or her sweet-ass time going through. It's just a door waiting to be used. It's begging to be used.

"Open me, please," it would say if it could talk. "I was just WD40ed this very morning!"

Just don't expect anyone to hold said door for you, and if you hold it for someone else, don't expect a thank-you either. Just do the right thing because it's what you do, and if someone appreciates it, all the better.

But be prepared, because you can fully expect a door to smack you in the face if you're not paying attention. Then again, there are millions of Oblivions who don't even think to hold the door for anyone. They got through, and that's all that really matters.

They're Oblivions, remember?

CLOTHES EVERYWHERE!

Now that you've finally made it through the doors in one piece and you're in your favorite department store, it's hard to actually get any shopping done. That's because you're too busy stepping over the piles of clothes that Oblivions and their hordes pulled off the shelves and never bothered to put back.

Now *you* have a hard time finding your size in the pile that was once neatly folded, because somebody rummaged through every single item to find exactly what *they* were looking for, not giving a second thought either to the person whose job it is to fold those clothes and make them presentable, or to the next shopper who deserves to look through a neat pile of clothes, just like they did.

To make matters worse, these inconsiderate Oblivions will justify to themselves and to anybody who would dare call them out with some lame old, tired excuse like: "It's not my job to fold the sweaters."

What they're really saying is screw you and screw the employees. Why should they care? They satisfied *their* needs, didn't they?

People are rude.

It's as simple as that. But don't let that stop you from going out to the malls. Just know it going in. It's like going to see a Tom Arnold movie. You don't go to a Tom Arnold movie and expect it to be good. You go because you're out of town visiting family and you just have to get away, and not even a Tom Arnold flick can keep you from your much-needed escape. (Sorry, Tom. You're a great guy, but your movies suck.)

THE FRAGRANCE DEPARTMENT

Every department store has a fragrance department, usually located at the mall entrance. This is so the competing smells of hundreds of different brands of colognes, sprays, perfumes, and creams can assault your nostrils and pierce your brain, giving you an eye headache as soon as you walk in.

It's the department store's way of saying, "Welcome, shoppers!"

To top it off, as if Obsession for Men and Drakkar Noir aren't bad enough, there's inevitably some man or woman whose job it is to get you to sample the newest Tommy Hilfiger scent. They stand there with sample cards and spray bottles at the ready, modern day gunslingers just waiting to ambush you as you make your way through Dodge City.

"Obsession for Men? Obsession for Men?"

It sounds more like a statement but the raised eyebrows of the staffers indicate that if you're indeed interested, just stop where you are. Shoppers do their best not to make eye contact with these folks, because as a whole, shoppers are weak at heart. We'll go ahead and sample the cologne if we make eye contact. It's a non-Oblivion trait to give others the benefit of the doubt.

The staffer then sprays their scent of the day on a sample card, wave it like a wand in the air, and then stick it under your nose.

But here's the kicker. By the time you sniff the sample your nostrils are fried. Walking through the fragrance department is like sniffing hydrochloric acid. Your nose is bleeding by the time you hit the mall.

I tried using that excuse once as some nice young lady strategically stepped in front of me and urged me with her pretty blue eyes to try the latest scent. Yeah, I'm a sucker for a cutie.

"I can't smell anything right now. Too many smells," I said, trying to get away as subtly as possible.

She immediately whipped out a little glass container filled with coffee beans and stuck one in my face.

"Sniff this, it will will clear your nostrils," she said. I should have hired her to sell Grrr! T-shirts. She was good, but in the end, I managed to escape with my credit card firmly in my wallet, knowing that my Old Spice and Paul Sebastian (both colognes I can get at a drugstore), were safe for another few weeks.

Besides, I like smelling like a man.

THE METROSEXUAL

There's something a little girly about the whole metrosexual phenomenon. Sure, I would like to have a face as soft as a baby's ass, but I don't have forty-five minutes every morning to apply just the right concoction of prewash moisturizer followed by an oatmeal scrub and then a daily pick-me-up mud mask—all before applying a $45 shaving cream named after the history of aerospace, running a $4 triple-action blade slid into my $250 nickel-plated "shaving utensil" (but I know guys, the weight really helps . . . keep telling yourself that), and then another moisturizing aftershave—all in all a morning routine that I need to put as a line item into my monthly budget.

When I was growing up, one of my fondest memories was of my father splashing his Old Spice aftershave on his face. I used to love the

way the scent lingered in the bathroom even after my UPS man dad was long gone for work. For some reason that scent made his life seem romantic to me. Believe it or not, a memory like that can shape who you are for the rest of your life.

Somehow, I don't think the sight of Dad wearing a mud mask would have had the same effect on me.

YOU ARE HERE

Malls are so big these days it's hard to find what you're looking for. That's why there are maps conveniently located in various high-trafficked spots.

So you mosey on over to try to find the "You Are Here" dot and then figure out where it is you're going and what route you need to get there.

Except that there is always some Oblivion standing right in front of the map, as if it were there solely for her, isn't there? So you clear your throat a few times until this Obliviot wanders off, because God knows she didn't even notice you were trying to see the map, too. Heaven forbid. That would have snapped her out of her "me, me, me" Oblivion trance, and we all know that's not going to happen.

So you finally find where it is you need to go (funny how you managed to do that while standing to the side of the map so that others can see, too, isn't it?), but you see that your destination is on another level.

So you're confronted with two choices: The escalator or the elevator?

This is probably an easy choice, because there's usually just one old, slow-moving elevator, and you know it's going to be filled with families with strollers or wheelchairs, so you opt to use the escalator.

Escalators are great inventions. Sometimes they are just what the doctor ordered for your tired legs and feet after a long day of shopping. But other times they're perfect for when you're in a rush, because you know most people follow the same rules of the road when riding escalators:

Keep Right, Pass Left. Right?

Well, not exactly. Unfortunately the Oblivions will stand two wide on the escalator, thus preventing anybody from getting by. Of course, the same two people will stop short at the bottom of the escalator, debating the pros and cons of the Johnny Rockets burger for lunch. Meanwhile, people are piling up behind them as the escalator deposits riders into their backs. It usually takes all of my energy to prevent me from plowing through them like Jerome Bettis going in for a touchdown. God knows if I even so much as brush them, they'll shoot me dirty looks, because of course it will be *my* fault.

These escalator hogs are also the same people who walk in front of you at a snail's space, four across and holding hands. Yeah, everybody else here is on their schedule and their shopping pace.

VELOUR SWEATSUITS

What's with these velour sweatsuits that everybody's wearing these days? I lost count of the number of people, young and old, who were strolling through the mall like Tony Soprano in these overpriced duds with sports insignias emblazoned all over the fabric. And the outfit apparently is incomplete without lots of gold chains, big hair, and oversized diamonds attached to the wearer.

Now, the men who wear these sweats usually wear them baggy with their sneakers untied. You know, the ultimate sign of hipness, class, and wealth, right?

But the women, for crying in the bucket! They wear these things at least one size too small, so the pants are too tight and reveal a thong strap, and the top just happens to leave room for the belly button ring to be exposed.

Now I'm as red-blooded as any man, but is this supposed to be attractive or unique?

THE FOOD COURT

And then there's the food court. Normally I avoid any restaurant whose food choices are pictured on the wall behind the counter, but that's just me. Sometimes you just have to have a burger or a Chinese buffet, I know that.

Of course you'll regret it later, but that's what Alka Seltzer was invented for.

But the people in the food court, from the clerks to the patrons, are collectively the biggest bunch of Oblivions you'll find at the mall. Don't you just love it when one person in a group runs over to the last empty table at the food court and grabs it while the rest of his or her group hits the Chik-Fil-A to put in their orders?

Meanwhile, there you are, walking around like a zombie trying to find a place to light, tray precariously in one hand trying to balance the food and drinks, a few shopping bags in the other hand and the kids in tow.

When you finally spot a table with empty seats there's usually somebody sitting there sheepishly, not making eye contact with anyone because he knows he's an Obliviot saving seats for his clan.

Being hungry in a mall is sure to make you Grrr! I tell people the two most Grrring factors are being too hungry or being too hot.

Hot *and* hungry is a lethal combination. I don't know about you, but when I'm hot and hungry at the same time, I become a madman. My wife calls me Malachi from *Children of the Corn* at those moments. Those are the times when I start calling out the Oblivions. I mean, usually I just observe them. But hot and hungry? Watch out.

STARBUCKS

So you've been in the mall for an hour and you've managed to purchase a sweater or a pair of jeans, but you've got a caffeine headache. The Starbucks coffee shop is just what the doctor ordered. The line of course is long, because everybody gets a caffeine headache in the mall—or at the very least, everybody has a headache and thinks a shot of caffeine will do the trick.

Never mind the fact that the reason everybody has a headache is due to the Oblivions, and sadly, Starbucks is an Oblivion Magnet.

You can be standing in line for ten whole minutes, and the Oblivion in front of you, having had ten minutes to make up his mind, won't know what he wants. He'll just hem and haw until finally deciding on a cup of coffee—no wait—he's going for the grande macchiato with skim milk and whipped cream—no wait—what is a Frappaccino after all?

Oblivion: "Is the grande a large?"

Clerk: "No, it's a medium. We have tall, grande, and venti."

Oblivion: "But *grande* means 'large.' "

Clerk: "I don't know. It's how we do it."

Oblivion: "Why not just say small, medium, and large? Why is the small tall? It doesn't look tall to me. The venti looks tall. Why not short, medium, and tall, instead of tall, grande, and venti?"

Clerk: "I just work here."

Of course, after taking the order and not knowing why Starbucks has a strange naming convention for its various sizes, the customer is still expected to leave a tip.

Leave a tip for a cup of coffee to go?

TIPPING

Tipping in this country has gotten out of control. You can't pump your own gas anymore without leaving a tip for the person inside monitoring the pumps, for crying out loud. If you go to a casino and lose your shirt playing blackjack, well, you should take that last five bucks out of your wallet and leave it for the dealer, because he wants a tip, too.

You know, tipping is customary "to insure prompt service," hence the term *tips*. Collectively, there is a lot that I'm willing to tip for. And there is a lot that I cannot do.

Open heart surgery looks particularly hard. Ditto brain surgery, rocket science, heck, even simple algebra is over my head, and if it were customary to tip my doctor for saving my life, I'd be a decent tipper.

But one thing I do know how to do, and very well, I might add—all by myself—is go to the bathroom. So when I walk into a men's room at a fancy steak house or club, the last thing I need is help. I don't need mouthwash, or Drakkar Noir, or even a stick of gum.

And I certainly don't need someone to pump the handle on the paper towel dispenser three or four times for me. In short, I have no use for the bathroom valet.

None.

I don't want your cologne, or your Scope, or your Doublemint gum. I don't even want your "How you doin'?" I just want to use the facilities in peace. I don't want to be guilted into throwing a dollar into your tip jar.

I shouldn't have to give you money for something I can do very well on my own, and I shouldn't have to tip in order to use a clean restroom at a restaurant. These places certainly charge a lot of money for menu items, so the least they can do is keep the bathroom presentable at no extra cost, don't you think? Besides, I'd rather give that money to my server or my sommelier. I need help in getting my food from the kitchen to my table. I'd like someone else to go into the wine cellar and retrieve the bottle I ordered, bring it to my table, pop the cork, and then pour it into my glass.

But help in the john? No, thank you. Don't want it. Didn't request it. Don't even want to think about it.

It's bad enough that most bathrooms can barely fit two people as it is, I don't need to be squeezing by the valet getting in and out. Nope. Not interested. No, siree.

And how does one apply for the job as the bathroom valet anyway? Do you think they walk in to a club or a restaurant with a resume full of references for the job? How does one even request the position?

"No, Mr. Manager, not interested in waiting on tables, cooking or even busing tables. What I really want to do is spend six hours in the men's room handing out paper towels and sticks of bubble gum to men who are in dire need of a urinal. Now that's how I want to contribute to society."

I don't really get it.

And then there's that awkward moment when you use the bathroom for a second time. You feel the need to announce loudly enough for everyone else to hear that you were already there and "I got you last time."

Not to mention that the last thing I'm thinking about as I'm heading to the facility is bringing my wallet with me, "for the bathroom valet." Heck, I barely carry cash anymore as it is. Next thing you know the valet will have a credit card machine for tips.

So to the bathroom valet, the concept of the bathroom valet, the nightclubs and restaurants that employ the bathroom valet and the society that makes the bathroom valet even conceivable, I say, "Grrr!"

And the same goes for leaving a tip for coffee to go.

You ever wonder why a cup of java costs a buck and change these days? So you can say "keep the change." It's so you drop two bucks on a cup of coffee because you feel guilted into dropping the change in the coffee mug in front of the counter labeled TIPS.

Even the Indian and Middle Eastern families who own every Dunkin Donuts shop on the East Coast latched on to the American tipping frenzy.

"Box of Munchkins and a medium coffee, please. Keep the change."

Now, at a diner, where you sit at the counter, and a waitress comes over, puts a napkin on the counter, pours you a cup of coffee, delivers it to you along with cream, sugar, and a spoon, I can understand leaving a tip.

But at Starbucks—or other gourmet coffee shops—you're served your tasty beverage in a paper cup with a top on it. You're forced to find the cream and sugar at some stand somewhere in the shop (they're never in the same place), remove the lid, pour some coffee in the trash can because there's never enough room for cream and sugar, put the accoutrements in yourself, and still leave a tip.

I don't get it.

It's one thing to pay a premium for good coffee. It's one thing to pay a premium because Starbucks offers health benefits and a 401(k) plan to its employees. But to leave a tip on top of that premium for service that usually doesn't require a tip is beyond me.

And I'm an excellent tipper. (Although they say overtipping is a sign of insecurity. Who, me?)

Imagine your World War II–era grandparents seeing a tip jar at a coffee shop. They would probably figure it to be a "leave a penny, take a penny" feature and use it when they came up short a few cents for their purchase.

THE GIFT CARD

Don't be surprised when you try to use your Starbucks gift card to pay for your venti beverage, only to be told by the tip-soliciting counter clerk that this is not an actual Starbucks, but a licensee or whatever it is, and they can't accept that Christmas gift that's been sitting in your wallet these past few months.

Why bother buying gift cards at all if you can't use them everywhere you see a Starbucks sign? It's like when the idiots who run Blockbuster Video advertised "the end of late fees," after making you pay them for so long because you were five minutes late in returning the tape.

Anyway, Blockbuster franchises didn't have to participate in the no-late-fee deal, so customers who watched the commercials and heard the radio jingles thought that it was now okay to be five minutes late ended up being charged anyway.

National chains should require all licensees or franchises to accept any corporate endeavor when it relates to the customer. Surely Starbucks, being a Seattle-based company where Microsoft is located, can hire a few programmers to ensure that the money from the gift card gets allocated to the proper store, owned and operated or not.

As a customer, I don't really care about the backroom financials of my local coffee shop. If the sign says STARBUCKS, I should be able to use a gift card. If the sign says BLOCKBUSTER, then, by golly, I shouldn't be charged a late fee after I'm told, "Hey, look here, suckers-who've-been-ripped-off-by-us-for-so-long-because-we-were-the-only-game-in-town-until-some-little-company-called-Netflix-came-around-and-stole-all-of-our-disgruntled-customers, we're not charging late fees anymore!"

But I digress.

Now, after all of that, you still have a headache—because the idiot in front of you held you up; you weren't sure which size word meant what size because, after all, English is your first language; you couldn't use your gift card because you weren't actually at a Starbucks, even though the big green sign says STARBUCKS; you had to bring the cream container up to the counter—to ask someone to refill it because it was empty—and were guilted into leaving a tip after you got a huff from the barista because you interrupted her.

But hey, at least you can enjoy your gourmet coffee now, right?

No, wait, not just yet. Yup, it's so hot that you'll have to wait at least twenty minutes before you can actually drink it.

Isn't the mall grand? Or should that be "venti"?

MANNEQUINS

Good thing the FCC doesn't have any jurisdiction over shopping malls. If so, I'm sure retail stores would be heavily fined for displaying clothes on mannequins that sport protruding nipples.

As if we men weren't already sex-obsessed enough, now we're doing double takes at plastic renditions of the female form.

THE CHECKOUT COUNTER

Some people have credit problems. This doesn't make them bad people. In fact, I once had a credit card rejected and I started laughing. I said, "Oops, try this one instead." The waiter at the restaurant where this happened was pleasantly surprised that I didn't pull the old "that's got to be a mistake; try it again" bit.

Look, folks, it's rare that there's an issue at the store. Perhaps your bank has the issue, or you know darn well why your card was rejected. But rest assured, nobody around you will judge you poorly. It's happened to all of us, so don't go on and on about how your card couldn't possibly be rejected, forcing the clerk to hand a phone over the counter so you can plead your case to the credit card company.

All the while you're holding up the people in line behind you.

And then there are the ones who are returning practically everything they ever bought, right before you, of course, and right after the second clerk just went on her break. So you start to look around for another register that has a shorter line but there never is one, so you're stuck.

I always get uncomfortable when I hear patrons yell at counter clerks, especially when whatever the problem is, is the fault of the Oblivion patrons themselves. This happens when the patron hands over a 20-percent-off coupon and never bothered to look at the date. Whether it's expired or the sale has yet to begin, these Oblivions think that yelling at the clerk will help them get their 20 percent off.

But that doesn't excuse the fact that there are several, several, several counter clerks out there who just don't give a damn. They don't care about you. They don't care about their employer. They don't care about themselves. These people are so bad at their jobs it looks like they are deliberately trying to get fired so that they can collect unemployment checks.

There's nothing worse than encountering a crappy store clerk. Here you are spending your hard-earned money so that people can have jobs, doing what you need to do to stimulate the economy, and you're forced to deal with some Obliviot.

Did I mention I love going shopping?

6

It's the Service, Stupid!

On a recent holiday shopping excursion, my wife and I decided to hit one of the several chain restaurants that can be found around most malls in America.

After waiting the customary hour to be seated, our table was not yet cleaned or set, and evidence of the young children who had dined in the booth before us lay at our feet in the form of smashed French fries. After more than ten idle minutes, a harried server finally made an appearance to take our order and didn't return with our drinks for another ten.

Needless to say, our dining experience did not get off to a good start. But alas, it is what we've come to expect when dining at such establishments these days.

Now comes news that the restaurant industry is hungry for business. Should this surprise anybody?

Clearly, something is not sitting well with American diners.

So what is it that's turning people off? Is it the economy? Is it the ads? I don't think so. It's bad service.

When I was a kid, one of my first jobs was working as a bicycle mechanic at Roy's Bike Shop. Roy gave me this advice on being a valuable employee: "Treat the business like it was your own."

These days consumers are hard-pressed to encounter service industry professionals in the larger retail and food chains who treat the business as if they owned it. There is very little sense of pride in the workplace anymore, where underpaid or, more accurate, undertrained staffs serve as poor representations of their employers' principles.

There are no winners in this scenario. Investors lose value as stock prices fall, workers lose jobs or are paid lower wages when business is bad, upper management is replaced under pressure from Wall Street, and consumers get shoddy service.

Good service does not come without sacrifice.

Employees have to develop a "customer first, me second" mentality, and conversely, companies have to work hard to set an example and properly train employees.

Terrie Dort, a president of the National Council of Chain Restaurants, told me during a phone interview that blaming the decline in business on bad service is way too simplistic. "It's the shift in competitive forces," says Dort, who also points her finger at home meal replacements, where consumers buy prepared meals from specialty stores to eat at home.

"They are entering the marketplace in a way they have never before, and newer concepts are muscling in on more established franchises," she said.

I don't buy it, but if I did, I'd still say it's the bad service that forces me to seek out alternatives such as prepared meals or online shopping.

I HATE MY JOB

Now, to be fair, no amount of training or supervision can protect a retail store or restaurant from the employee who simply hates his job. More than likely this person not only hates his job, but he hates his mother, his father, his sister, his brother, his dog, his cat, his neighbor, himself . . . you get the idea.

Some workers deserve to have the living crap beat out of them, but, of course, that's exactly what they're hoping you do, preferably if you're famous or otherwise wealthy, so that they can sue you for everything you have and never work another day in their useless lives.

Sadly, these people invade our malls and our restaurants with blind abandon. They are the Oblivions behind the counters, and they are out to ruin your day.

There's nothing we can do about these people. You can't complain about them to the floor manager, because it only makes *you* look like an Obliviot. You can't just take it, because then you won't be able to look at yourself in the mirror.

What you can do is leave. Leave the merchandise on the counter and just walk away. If you haven't ordered your meal yet, just get up and leave. If you have ordered it, walk to the front, pay for your drinks and cancel your dinner order, citing "unprofessional service."

You don't have to take shit. So don't.

WHEN BLACK FRIDAY COMES

Now, when writing a column called the "Grrr!" it's hard to take one's self all too seriously.

It's only a matter of time when the Grrrinch will come down the mountain and steal my Christmas; so until then, I give thanks to all of you who actually read my column. I know you'd be lost without it—*not*.

But the same could be said for all of us in our careers, couldn't it?

Seriously, who among us is 100 percent indispensable in his job? Unless you own a private company where you alone know the business, you would be hard-pressed to find someone out there who couldn't be replaced in a heartbeat.

But that's just your company. There's probably a competitor who would gladly take your clients if you faltered, and those clients wouldn't miss you in the least. Just ask any former hardware store owner who's working at the local Home Depot or Lowes.

So if you think about it, no matter how much you may despise your job, you should be thankful you have it. Look on the bright side: At least you don't work for GM.

Right before Christmas 2005, General Motors laid off thousands of workers, just in time for the holidays. Nice. Meanwhile, stockbrokers and other Wall Street sharks were the happy recipients of some of the biggest year-end bonuses since the 1990s. We're talking millions of dollars in a bonus, often more.

And guess what? Those self-absorbed Wall Street sharks will complain that it wasn't enough, and you know what? They're probably right, considering how much money they're bringing into the fold.

Ask yourself as you open your measly Christmas bonus—or lack thereof—*Why didn't I go to Wall Street?*

But the rich and powerful aren't the only ones lamenting their good fortune—eh-hum—I mean, hard times.

When Black Friday—the day after Thanksgiving—and the holiday shopping season is upon us, we should note that retail employees—for the most part—are good, hard-working people. Oftentimes they are subjected to the rudest Oblivions among us while coping with not-so-great working conditions. Most big-box retailers don't offer health benefits, retirement plans, or paid vacation time.

On top of that, some shoppers are so narrow-minded that they actually believe with all their might that the person behind the counter or sweeping the shopping center floors or folding clothes is seriously there just to serve them. And those Oblivion shoppers treat those retail workers like doo-doo.

On the flip side, there are the clerks who look at you with dread and insincerely state, "Can I help you?"

Well, actually, no, I'm just standing here holding an armful of merchandise *for my health.*

These people should be taken out to the mall loading docks, lined up, and fired, one by one.

That's why I make it a point to be nice to retail clerks this time of the year—if they look like they're doing the best they can at their jobs. We all know the ones we're talking about here. They know who they are, too.

In case you're wondering what kind of clerk you are, take the following quiz.

1. When driving to work do you:
   A. Sing Christmas carols?
   B. Pretend to run over shoppers with your car?
   C. Think of ways to look too busy to help people?

2. When standing behind the counter do you:
   A. Grind your teeth?
   B. Smile and take pride in doing your job?
   C. Sigh loudly when another person gets in line?

3. When approached by a customer do you:
   A. Picture them bleeding from the ears?
   B. Wish they would drop dead?
   C. Be as helpful and kind as you can be?

If you answered 1A, 2B, and 3C, you're in for a great month of holiday shopping and overtime, and you should know that your shoppers and your employers appreciate your efforts. It's people like you who are first to dish out holiday cheer to your community.

That's seriously a big deal, and most of us are thankful to you for that.

However, if you answered anything else, don't fret, because you're in good company. That's exactly how the Oblivion shoppers feel when they look at you, too.

You deserve each other.

Random Customer Service Grrr!

One day I called my home security company about a problem with my home security panel. (We've had so many issues my wife knows the number by heart, but I digress.) The woman in customer service with whom I spoke told me that my problem was a result of a limitation with the type of panel that we have, and we would have to upgrade my service. I hung up, aggravated. After a few seconds, I decided her solution was unacceptable to me, so I called back with the intention of canceling my home security system if they couldn't meet my request. This time, however, I got through to a different customer service rep, who told me my existing panel could be reprogrammed to do what I wanted it to do in the first place, at no extra charge. So I didn't need to grind my teeth after all!

Now, in case you're wondering if you're an Oblivion shopper, here's a quiz for you.

1. When you drive to the mall do you:
   A. Think about how much money you're wasting on gifts for people you don't really like?
   B. Look forward to finding and buying some great gifts?
   C. Wonder if you'll have enough time to get home to watch your soap?

2. When you approach a retail worker do you:
   A. Look right through them?

B. Belittle them with demands instead of kind requests?

C. Notice how hard they're working on such a busy shopping day, recognize that they may have had a job just like yours and that now they're doing what they have to do to make ends meet, and so you greet them with kindness and respect?

3. When you spend your hard-earned cash do you:
   A. Grrrind your teeth?
   B. Organize your budget in your head?
   C. Complain to the clerk about how much you just spent?

If you answered 1B, 2C, and 3B, you're going to have a smooth shopping season. If you answered anything else, well, just like the previous quiz, there's a clerk out there just waiting to give it right back to you.

But here's a simpler way of looking at it. If you're shopping for gifts for people, chances are you or someone in your family has a job. You should be thankful.

And if you're working at the stores where people are shopping, you too have a job. Chances are you take pride in that job, and you should be thankful.

It's easy to forget the meaning of the Thanksgiving holiday.

7

The Mile High Grrr! Club:
Something Grrring in the Air

Air travel, from airports to airlines to travelers and staffers, makes up a lot of Grrring moments in our lives.

From the little kid kicking the back of your seat while his Oblivion parents are paying no mind, to the same little brat watching *Finding Nemo* on his DVD player at full volume—without headsets—air travel has seen better days.

I was on a flight from Atlanta to Honolulu to cover the Pro Bowl one year. The genius behind me put a Lap Saver on the back of my seat so that I could not recline. Now, being a non-Oblivion, I don't lie in the lap of the person behind me in coach. But come on, dude, I am not flying nine and a half hours without reclining, even a little.

Being savvy to why my seat would not go back, I simply turned around, confirmed he had the lap saver clips on the seat, and said, "You've got to be kidding me. Take those things out." And he did, without a word.

But I can understand why he has them. Some people will just lay all the way back in their chair with absolutely no regard for the person behind them.

In this post–Sept. 11 world, I've resigned myself to taking early flights—as early as they depart. Six A.M.? I'm on it. That's because I know security is a headache, and I don't really like dealing with crowds (who does?). But still, people will wait until the last minute to get to the airport, and then huff and puff and look at their watches and be rude to the ticket agents and security guards because they have to wait and "Don't you know my flight leaves in ten minutes?"

People who are late arriving for their flights should immediately be bumped to the next available flight—*available* being the operative word. After watching several flights depart to their destinations, it's pretty guaranteed that the Airport Oblivions will get the message. Now I have a lot of Grrrs toward the airlines in general, not the least of which is sitting next to a person who paid a quarter of what you paid for the same flight, or the clowns who get bumped to first class because they made enough noise about getting an upgrade.

Personally, I don't mind coach. It gives me plenty to Grrr! about.

But even before I get on a plane I more than likely have Grrred a good ten times. From the people who do not know how to use the e-ticket self-check-in to the ones who feign complete surprise that they have to pay $50 extra when their bag weighs more than 75 pounds, people never, ever learn.

Because they're Oblivions.

You see, Oblivions are so busy worrying about themselves at all times that they never learn from their mistakes, and they are never observant enough to learn through osmosis.

At the security line they just have to try their luck. So they don't take their shoes off, only to be sent back to the conveyor belt to deposit them. Then their belt buckle sets off the machine, and we have to hear how "it never set it off before." Yeah, okay.

Of course, these same Oblivions use six bins for their stuff, not thinking that their wallet and cell phone can actually fit in the same bin. And don't even get me started on what they do on the other side of the metal detector, when they stand there and repack all their crap.

They refuse to wait until their number is called, and they'll congregate at the gate so that you, the person who can actually board now, has to walk through them. I like to use a little shoulder to make my point.

At least one Oblivion will keep boarding passengers waiting while she tries to stuff her too-large carry-on into the overhead bin. Then she'll take even longer to empty half of it into her personal bag so it'll fit in the bin.

If they're lucky enough to have all three seats in a row on a long flight, it's not enough that they can relax and spread out. They usually like to lay supine, with their disgusting bare feet hanging over the aisle.

Pet lovers have it rough on planes, I'll give you that. Nobody wants to check their pets, but sometimes you just have to, especially if you know your little kitty or pooch is a bad traveler. And you know you know that your pet is a bad traveler. Don't sit there and act all surprised when the dog craps in his carrier or the cat squeals bloody murder for the entire flight.

I had the pleasure of sitting in a twosome with a little hottie who, of course, had a little terrier—or as I like to call them, a living, breathing accessory. At first I thought I'd hit the jackpot. Even though I'm off the market, I'm not going to argue about sitting next to a hot chick for a six-hour flight to Los Angeles. But God punished me for my impure thoughts; the chick's little doggie peed and crapped all over her little dog purse, and the stench was not fun to deal with, especially when the snack box arrived.

But even still, the smell wasn't as bad as the dog's incessant whining, which lasted the entire flight. I wanted to strangle the dog and the girl before the flight was over.

Serves me right. Also, would it be so hard for airlines to program enough music on any given channel of its in-flight music offering so that you won't hear the same loop every half hour? How hard can that be?

Just a Little Off the Top . . . Grrr!

What's the difference between a good haircut and a bad haircut?

About two weeks.

You ever go into the barbershop or beauty salon and know exactly what you want, only to have your hair butchered beyond anything resembling, well, you? I Grrr! beauticians who think they know what's best for their clients more than their clients do.

Of course, there are those who walk into a beauty salon and surrender themselves freely to the whims of their stylist. That's fine for those people. I, for one, go into my barbershop and like to tell them exactly what I want—high and tight, and not too much off the front. Inevitably I get some scissor-happy barber who is hell-bent on making me look like John Candy in *Stripes.*

8

Self-Righteons and Other Self-Absorbed Know-It-Alls Who Need To Get Over Themselves

You're sober. Congratulations. Now let me buy you a nice tall glass of Shut-the-Hell-Up.

I don't mean to diminish the importance of cleaning up one's act. Conquering a demon as powerful as alcoholism is truly a feat.

But that doesn't mean everyone around you has to know that you don't drink, or you're sober now, in that I-take-myself-very-seriously tone. Such a statement is always met with something along the lines of "Well, good for you," in some faux enthusiastic tone in and of itself.

Just shut up.

Seriously, just what is the purpose of announcing to your coworker or new friend that you're sober? "But Alcoholics Anonymous teaches us to do that." Blah blah blah. Shut up. Why not just say "No thanks" to the drink? No explanation is needed, unless of course you're talking about a very close friend, or someone you'd like to be close friends with. Surely the guy who has you out on a sales call shouldn't qualify.

And even when some Obliviot won't take no for an answer and insists on buying you a drink, why not just order a Coke or a seltzer with lime?

The Grrr! here is when sobriety becomes the recovering alcoholic's very identity. Believe it or not, there are millions of recovering alcoholics who don't wear their personal mission on their sleeves.

An *Entertainment Tonight* profile on *Lost* star Naveen Andrews revealed to viewers that he is a recovering heroin addict and an alcoholic. "In England everyone hangs out in pubs," he said, explaining how he came to be addicted to alcohol. The piece was chock-full of inside information about his personal fight, and ultimate conquest of his addictions. The gorgeous reporter in the miniskirt and boots ended her report by thanking him for being so honest with her.

Thanks for being honest with you? Sweetheart, he should be thanking you for the publicity. "I have an idea, Mr. Agent. Why don't we send out a press release on how rock bottom I was before I became rich and famous. That should grab—hook, line, and sinker—some little hot reporter looking to make a name for herself and get me some duly needed press."

Andrews spread the same message on the talk show circuit—*The Tony Danza Show* among them. Talk about desperate.

I guess I should feel happy that not only was he an Emmy-nominated millionaire actor on the Disney-owned ABC network, but he's also a rehabilitated drug addict.

"Good for him," I said enthusiastically to the television screen. You see, I'm happy now that he's made it. I wasn't happy before, but now that I know he was a down-on-his-luck druggie before he became famous, well then, more power to him! Puhleez!

But the Grrr! is not just reserved for the self-righteous rehabilitated alcoholic.

The gym-going diet-conscious person is worse. He or she is the person who walks by your desk at work just as you're opening the Wendy's bag and snidely remarks, "Wendy's. That's a real healthy lunch."

Really? Well, who asked you? Do you really believe I care what you think of my dieting habits? Are you that self-absorbed to think that I would be guilted into throwing my Biggie fries into the trash and going out for a salad just because the office fitness pro has his eye on me?

Gyms are full of exercise nuts eager to explain how to curl your arm *just so,* so that your bicep gets that most desired baseball shape and hardness.

Thanks for the insight, Conan The Barbarian, but we're okay. We like our muscles to have purpose, grace, and elegance. You know, long and lean muscle, like an athlete. I don't know what you do for a living, Conan, but not all of us can afford a new wardrobe every time our neck or back goes up another size.

Here's a hint, oh master of the gym: unless you're depositing a check with my name on it and the words "personal training" written on the memo line, I'm not interested in your help.

Ex-smokers tend to be annoying as hell, too.

These people smoked for twenty years, and since they've finally kicked their habit, everyone around them who smokes is killing them with secondhand smoke. Again, please! Like the emissions from the daily traffic jam on Sixth Avenue won't kill you first?

Yes, *tsk-tsk* them to death. Meanwhile, it was people like you who peer-pressured these now heavily addicted smokers into taking up smoking to begin with.

"Have a cigarette, it'll make you look cool."

These *tsk*ers are too self-centered to realize that by harping on their sobriety or nicotine conquests, they are behaving in the same dangerous and addictive manner that put them in harm's way in the first place, to say nothing of the pure self-absorption.

Incidentally, why should they be so proud about acting normal? Nobody pats you on the back when you pay your bills, take care of your children, or save money for rainy days, do they? It's like Chris Rock said about black men in the ghettos who say they take care of their kids. "You're supposed to, you dumb mother—!" Rock counters.

Grow up.

One person who e-mailed the "Grrr!" column told me he once witnessed a young mother purchase a box of diapers, a box of baby wipes, and two packs of Marlboros. When she came up a few dollars short, she left the baby wipes at the register and went her merry way with her cigarettes.

The e-mailer commented sarcastically that the young woman wouldn't want to go easy on the smokes and stretch out one pack until she could raise the five bucks for a second pack, now would she? Nah, the baby can go with a dirty bottom instead.

Unbelievable. But then again, I'm sure she'd say "Who asked you?" to the guy who would comment. Maybe she just remembered that she has a box of baby wipes at home, and she could wait another week. Who are we to judge? Was he a Self-Righteon? I don't know. That's a tough one to consider. I would bet that he is. But then again, she could be an Obliviot unfit mother too.

But I digress (something I do often). Back to the Self-Righteons.

At work, besides the office gym rat, you've also got the busybody who constantly offers unsolicited help. For example, your cubicle neighbor overhears the tongue-lashing you've just received from the boss, and she comes over to whisper about how you should maneuver the political minefield in the office.

Seriously, who asked you? And while we're talking, stop listening to all my private conversations. Don't you have a job to do? Nobody likes a busybody, unless of course you've got juicy gossip about someone else. Then you're tolerable for at least a few minutes.

More Unsolicited Advice

Women know the married guy who likes to give unsolicited advice to them on how to deal with men. If you've got a guy who loves to tell you how to deal with your man, chances are he's hitting on you. Don't believe that he's simply trying to help. It's his way of flirting, and it's cheesy.

Dude, go home to your wife. If you're not happy, get a divorce. It's that simple. Please spare the women your valuable insight. They're making fun of you. You ever notice how they roll their eyes as you're approaching? I didn't think so.

Because . . . you . . . are . . . an . . . Oblivion.

You can also count on unsolicited advice from the office voter police. You know the people who come in late on Election Day announcing that they observed their right to vote.

Yes, you did, and you were the only one, too. Guess what? We voted, too, and still managed to get to work on time. Come Ash Wednesday, there's always the people who make a point to visit everybody in the office—even people they don't have to deal with, just so everybody knows how observant a Catholic they are.

Self-Righteons. I'll tell you, they are everywhere. Some are well-intentioned, but you know what they say about the road to hell? It's paved with good intentions.

On the roads, Self-Righteons become Left Lane Vigilantes.

Left Lane Vigilantes
and Other Reasons Why
Road Rage Exists

Now, of course I don't advocate driving like maniacs on the highway. But there is such a thing as keeping up with the flow of traffic. And when the majority of drivers are traveling at 80 mph, it's not safe to decide you're going to be the lone holdout doing 65 mph in the fast lane.

Move over.

No, you're not doing us any favors. No, you're not keeping the roads safer than the rest of us. You are a nuisance, and a dangerous one at that, you self-righteous Obliviot, you Left Lane Vigilante.

Move over.

You're the type of person who crosses in front of a city bus because you have the right of way, and HE HAD THE RIGHT OF WAY is exactly what we'll write on your gravestone, too.

Which reminds me . . .

Isn't it odd how much trust we have in the assembly line workers and computer technicians who design, make, and install the brakes in our vehicles? We trust with our very lives (or the use of our arms and legs, anyway) that those moving vehicles will stop just before crushing us to death. I don't get it.

The same Nervous Nellies who stomp holes in the passenger-side floor by pounding on the imaginary brake when riding with their children drivers don't think twice about crossing the street illegally, in front of moving traffic. On top of that, they'll often stop in the middle of the street long enough to give dirty looks to drivers who dared not slow down for them.

But that's not to say that some drivers don't deserve the look.

I've long wanted to make a sign on a stick for drivers who realize they've made a mistake. On one side it reads I'M AN OBLIVION. In other words, "my bad" or "sorry about that." On the other side it reads YOU'RE AN OBLIVION. In other words, "get your head out of your ass."

I bet signs like that would reduce the number of road rage incidents.

Notice I said *number* of incidents, and not *amount* of incidents. That's another Grrr! Don't you just hate when people say *amount* when they mean *number*? Or *tons* when they describe how many people arrived at the antiwar protest? What, are you weighing them?

Self-Righteons are the types of drivers who will not, under any circumstances, let someone merge in front of them. And I'm not talking about the Obliviot who rides the left lane, zooming past the long line of cars at an exit, only to merge off the highway at the front of the line. That guy should be run off the road. I'm talking about when we're all stuck in the same traffic jam, and for the sake of moving, we have to let people merge in front of us. Most reasonable people understand that by not letting the car merge, by inching forward and squeezing him back in his or her lane, we're not gaining any ground whatsoever.

But Self-Righteons will risk denting their own cars just to prove they have the right of way.

How about when *you* make an Oblivion-type mistake on the road? Like, say, when you're making a left turn on a busy two-way road, and you have just enough time—based on the speed traveled by the cars you're about to turn in front of—to make your turn safely?

Don't you just love it when the person coming up behind you guns it and then rides up on your tailgate, all the while leaning on his horn? Dude, you were nowhere near me until you hit the gas. You're just looking for an excuse to be a Self-Righteon. Congratulations.

Boy, good thing you didn't hit me. Thank you for saving my life.

I had no idea how close you were. (I had no idea you were a Self-Righteon is more like it.)

Here's one for you that still boggles my mind.

Years ago I was driving a car with the ultimate Self-Righteon passenger. Now, I know that what I did goes against traffic laws—but I checked my mirrors and there was no danger. What did I do? I changed lanes in a solid-line area. However, what this Self-Righteon did went against any logic I can think of, and to this day the SR still thinks he was right.

When I put my blinker on and began to change lanes, the SR reached over, grabbed the steering wheel, and pulled the car back into the right lane. We could have crashed. And on top of the potential accident he could have caused, I thought that maybe there was a truck bearing down on top of me in the left lane that I didn't see.

You can imagine my confusion and hysteria in that one moment.

When I asked my passenger just what the hell he thought he was doing, he said, "You can't cross the solid line."

You can't cross the solid line? Dude, you can't drive the car from the passenger seat, either. Which infraction is worse? I crossed the solid line on a one-way highway when there was no car coming up behind me. He grabbed the steering wheel and pulled.

Still, to this day, he'll tell me I was wrong and he was right. Un-B-Lievable. That, my friends, is a Self-Righteon.

Yes, Dad, I'm talking about you, but I still love you . . . you Self-Righteon.

Of course not all bad drivers are Self-Righteons. Some are Obliviots.

THE POWER-HUNGRY COP

You know those cops who you can tell, just by looking at them, are going to bust your chops?

I encountered one such cop—a sheriff's deputy—one day when a

St. Patrick's Day parade was getting set to go down my block. As luck would have it, the deputy set up his roadblock exactly at my driveway.

I figured this should be pretty easy, and as I pulled up to his car, I put down the passenger-side window to let him know that I was going "right there" and pointed to my house.

"No, you're not!" the deputy screamed, and jumped out of his car with his nightstick in hand. He rushed over to the driver's side.

"Officer," I said, "I live right there." Again, I pointed to my driveway, which was about ten feet from where we were stopped.

"I don't care. The road is closed, and I don't know how you're going to get there," he said.

I really couldn't believe my ears.

"Dude, you're killing me," I said. "Do you mean to tell me that you will not let me drive another ten feet to my driveway? I live right there," I said, indicating my house for the third time.

Finally, the deputy said okay, but "just this once."

Unbelievable. Now I am a champion of law enforcement. Several of my friends are NYPD or New Jersey state troopers, so I know what they have to go through on a day-to-day basis. But even they will admit that there are guys who are just too immature for the job.

There are guys, like this sheriff's deputy, who are just looking to bust chops. These are the guys who—aside from the corrupt cops who break the law—give law-enforcement public servants a bad name.

Cops don't have to be your friends. We all know that. There is a time when cops must use force or be unwilling to bend because that's what the circumstances call for.

But not when a guy pulls up with a toddler and a wife in tow, looking to go another ten feet to get into his driveway, and all the cop is doing is directing traffic away from—*gasp*—a St. Patrick's Day Parade . . . that hasn't even started yet!

To put it kindly, this cop was a jerk.

He's the power-hungry guy who's on the job just to throw his weight around. He's the guy who's never going to cut anyone a break, even if the break is something as small as driving a few feet to get into one's driveway. I wonder what this sheriff's deputy's life was like growing up.

Did he have a Napoleon complex? Was he a victim of too much teenage acne? Or is he simply a jerk? Sadly, there's one or more like this guy on every police force throughout the world.

OBLIVIOTS

You know the Obliviot who refuses to use his turn signal, right? Don't you just love when he stops in the left lane to turn into the Wal-Mart? A little advance warning would have been nice so you wouldn't be stuck behind him as others zoom by you in the right lane (and God forbid they should let you in).

He is also zooming from lane to lane on the major highway without signaling.

And then there's the brake Obliviot. Sometimes she drives with both feet, so her brake lights are constantly on. But the real infraction occurs when she slams on her brakes because she sees a cop up ahead with somebody already pulled over.

Dude, he's busy. He's not going to decide in the middle of writing a speeding ticket that you would be a better summons and ditch the current job to give you chase. But thanks for allowing me and everybody else behind you to give our brakes a road test. It's good to know they're still working.

Now, one of the true Obliviot behaviorisms is the tossing of burning cigarette butts out of the car window. How many forest fires are started each year because some jackass didn't want to use his ashtray? Not to mention that these schmos justify littering by convincing themselves and everyone else that littering provides jobs for sanitation workers.

Yeah, and armed robbery provides jobs for cops, too.

Tourists are the worst drivers, because they don't know where they're going.

Rubberneckers will slow down to gawk at the fenderbender on the side of the road, meanwhile you're stuck in miles of traffic because they just can't mind their own business. Of course, since you're already going slow, you can't help but look, too.

We all do that.

Here's one of my favorite Oblivion moments. You pull over to the shoulder because a fire truck, an ambulance, or a cop car is heading to an emergency situation with sirens blaring and lights flashing, and some clown who has been traveling behind you passes you on the emergency vehicle's tail.

I wouldn't want to be a cop, especially a state trooper or a highway patrolman. Sure, the squad cars are cool and you get to speed and all, and the uniform is pretty awesome, but can you imagine busting chops day in and day out in the form of writing tickets to speeders? Yeah, I know speeding is wrong, but when the flow of traffic is 80 mph, how do the cops pick which car to pull over?

It's inherently a losing proposition. I'd much rather see the guy chasing the fire truck get the ticket. He and people like him are the real danger to society.

Here's one to add to the left-lane vigilantism that forces self-righteous slowpokes to ride in the left lane: People who don't let others merge.

Now, there are exceptions, like when some bozo rides the shoulder and then cuts into an already long lane. But there are other times when a driver should just let another car merge, for the sake of his own and other motorists' sanity.

For instance, oftentimes you may find yourself riding in a left lane that suddenly ends or is closed off for construction without any forewarning. You have no choice but to merge into the right lane. But there's always some person who simply refuses to let anyone merge in front of them. What is the big deal? People must merge eventually. It is a fact of life. *Let them in.* Grrr!

(((10)))

Grrrs in CyberSpace:
Internet Oblivions

Did you know that if you use a search engine, and look up, say, *Mike Straka*, you might come up with hundreds of thousands of pages. Most of them, however, would have more to do with hockey sensation Martin Straka, as opposed to your desired search.

But if you put your search in quotations, like *"Mike Straka,"* then only pages with that exact phrase will appear. This is simple stuff, folks, and it's as life-changing as the time you discovered the redial button on your telephone in the midst of a radio trivia question that you absolutely positively knew the answer to, and those U2 tickets were just one lucky phone call away.

Oblivions on the Internet range from folks who don't know how to search and usually wind up on some Web mall page that hijacks your home page and downloads spyware onto your hard drive and slows your computer to a snail's pace.

The Obliviots who run those types of sites are operating against the law, and eventually they'll get theirs. In the meantime, you need to learn how to navigate the Web, for your own protection.

One of the things that makes not only Internet users but also Internet companies particularly Grrring is the use of clever names for their companies. Names that have nothing to do with whatever it is the company is selling.

Avenue A/Razorfish? Do they fillet fish on party boats? No, they're an interactive marketing company. Hmmm. Okay.

Google? Well, we all know what they do.

Napster? How in the hell is one to determine what Napster is? Is it a sleep-aid drug?

Or how about *slurping*? This is a term for people who want to self-publish their blogs into books. You *slurp* up files in an iPod or similar device, and a software program automatically formats them in book form. And here I thought slurping was something Oblivions do with hot coffee and soup. Internet proprietors are hell bent on coming up with the most clever and ambiguous names for their companies, because in the go-go 1990s, when the Internet stocks went up like rockets, having a name that looked cool on the CNBC stock ticker was more important than creating a brand that consumers can identify with.

That's why we have eBay, the auction site that by name could be a virtual bay in cyberspace, for all we know. Xoom.com was an Internet portal, and Lycos was one of the first portals to focus on search. But for the life of me—at first glance, anyway—I have no idea what Lycos means. It sounds like a bathroom cleaner.

Spam mail is not only annoying in practice, the name was already a brand from Hormel. It's canned ham, and it should stay that way. Why not just call spam *junk e-mail*?

Red Hat is the Linux operating system champion, but you wouldn't know that by its name. At least Microsoft makes sense to its core business. Sun Microsystems makes sense. Apple doesn't make sense, although it makes damn good consumer products, and as it turns out, with its former animation unit Pixar, which was sold to Disney, it makes good movies too.

Phishing is a term used to describe identity thieves who send e-mails that look like genuine correspondence from banks to try to trick you into giving them your bank information so they can rob you blind. But if you only hear the term, you're thinking deep sea bass or the rock group.

Friendster and MySpace are good names of companies because they pretty much describe what those sites are all about, but Amazon.com? Amazon is a great online shopping mall, but the name conjures images of barracudas chomping at the bit.

Hollywood Insanity: Why Celebrities Are Ruining Our Country

TOM CRUISE IGNORES THE MEDIA

When it comes to generating media interest, Tom Cruise is an expert.

Ever since his divorce from the ultrasexy and ultratalented Nicole Kidman, it seems Cruise has made it his mission to be featured, talked about, written about, and photographed more than his Oscar-winning ex.

And he has succeeded.

In fact, when *Mission: Impossible 3* premiered in New York City, old Tomboy jetted around Manhattan by subway, by boat, by helicopter, and by fire engine to promote the J. J. Abrams–helmed action flick.

Do you think he did this because he was afraid none of us in the entertainment press would notice he had another movie coming out?

It's ironic, then, that at the Mexico City premiere of *M:I:III*, the world's biggest box-office draw claimed that he ignores all media reports about his personal life.

Even more ironic is that if the majority of Americans followed his lead, we'd all be better off. Ignoring those articles that deal with celebrities' personal lives would not only serve the stars' well-being but also our own. We would have to turn to literature to occupy that commuter train or bus ride home.

"Shakespeare for everyone," as Rodney Dangerfield said in his classic comedy *Back to School*. Maybe we'd actually have a conversation with a neighbor rather than burying our heads in some tabloid magazine full of paparazzi pics and made-up stories attributed to "close friends."

We wouldn't be rushing to the newsstand to buy *People* magazine so we can gawk at Angelina Jolie and Brad Pitt's daughter. We wouldn't be misled by dumbass headlines in *Star* magazine stating Jennifer Aniston was pregnant with Pitt's kid the same week they announced their divorce.

Star got another story wrong about Jessica Simpson and Nick Lachey. You'd think they would have learned . . .

But Cruise is full of it, anyway.

While he may personally ignore those articles that deal with his private life, he can't think that we are all so naïve as to think that those articles that deal with those portions of his life are not somehow even a little bit encouraged by him and his camp.

And why not? It is the Hollywood way, after all, especially where there's money to be made.

Did anybody besides Teri Hatcher's publisher, agents, and media handlers know that the Desperate Housewife had a book, *Burnt Toast*, coming out just weeks after she revealed in *Vanity Fair* that she was sexually molested by an uncle?

Yeah, I'm as jaded as they come, but sadly, this is the reality of the entertainment business, where even one of the most despicable crimes and abuse of trust can be used to help generate buzz.

In my opinion, Hatcher was in a lose-lose situation after coming out with the revelation that she was sexually abused. Yes, it was brave of her to confront the animal who abused her—and who may have caused one other girl to commit suicide—and as a result this monster is in jail for fourteen years.

For that we say thank you, Ms. Hatcher, and more victims of this type of abuse should report it to authorities.

But the fact that this story comes out in a cover story for *Vanity Fair* after its best-selling Oscar issue ever, featuring nude photos of Scarlett Johansson and Keira Knightley in what looked like a threesome with clothing designer Tom Ford on the cover, is a bit disingenuous, to say the least.

Hatcher was quoted in the article saying that she had thought about coming out with her story before but didn't want it to be tabloid fodder.

Okay . . . but it's all right to be *Vanity Fair* fodder?

Hatcher did what she had to do in order to put her evil uncle away; however, her story didn't need to be told to a mass audience. Isn't there anything sacred to celebrities? Is there not one thing they'd like to keep to themselves?

For my money, this would be one of those times.

Hatcher said she was worried that if she came out with her story before *Desperate Housewives* made her a household name, then she'd be subject to criticism from people thinking she was using that horrible experience for some much-needed publicity.

And she's right. But again, she's in a lose-lose situation.

Why do celebrities do this?

As if Lindsay Lohan doesn't get enough negative exposure from her troubled father, she has to confess to dabbling in drugs "a little" and battling bulimia.

(Lohan later denied having bulimia and said, "The words that I gave to the writer for *Vanity Fair* were misused and misconstrued, and I'm appalled with the way it was done." *Vanity Fair* stood by its story.)

Jane Fonda revealed in her book the sexual perversions of her first husband and how emotionally distant her famous father was toward her.

The list of "woe is me" millionaires goes on and on.

On the other hand, the only reason we know about Robert Downey Jr.'s drug problems is because a court ordered him into rehab. Downey Jr. didn't voluntarily enter a clinic for a shot in the publicity arm.

I know that these horrible experiences make people who they are. It makes them stronger and perhaps wiser, and probably better, actors.

But we all know someone who suffered something horrible in their lives. The difference is, they're not celebrities, so no magazines are asking them about it.

I for one don't want to hear any more personal junk from celebrities. I don't want to hear about their politics, and I don't want to hear about their sex lives or their vices. I don't care if Tom Cruise is gay or straight. I don't care that Ellen DeGeneres is dating Portia de Rossi, or if Sean Penn is a Democrat.

What I chiefly want to know about celebrities is this: Are you making a movie that I want to see? Are you in a television show that I want to record on my DVR, and is your next CD or single going to be catchy?

When I interview celebrities, I want to know about the work, the message of the film, and how they go about choosing or writing those scripts.

There was once a time when having a celebrity come out with postpartum depression like Brooke Shields, or child molestation like Hatcher, or drug use like Andrews, or HIV like Magic Johnson, to help us little people understand the dangers in the world, but it's been a long time since we've been that innocent.

These days, the reminders from celebrities are more than patronizing. They are insulting.

I'd be happy to believe Cruise about not paying attention to media reports about his personal life, but wasn't it he who announced to the world that he climbed the Eiffel Tower and proposed to Katie Holmes? Wasn't it he would jumped on Oprah's couch? Wasn't it he who announced the birth of his daughter, Suri?

I've defended Cruise in the past and, to some extent, will continue to do so. With the exception of his bizarre behavior and his unsolicited lectures on the values of Scientology, Tom Cruise is and always will be one of my favorite movie stars.

From *Risky Business* to *All The Right Moves* to *Top Gun*, Cruise has brought millions of people unabashed entertainment. In *Magnolia* and *Born On the Fourth of July*, he proved he can act.

In *Jerry Maguire,* he brought a character arc to the title role that was immediately identifiable by millions of American men.

Come to think of it, Tom Cruise's make-believe life is far more interesting than his personal one. It's no wonder he ignores those reports. Maybe we should all follow his lead.

After *M:I:III* opened, there was a *GQ* magazine featuring Cruise on the cover, and inside there was a long profile of the star, including pictures of him driving a vintage automobile and posing in a shirt and tie in the desert.

There was a time not so long ago that I would have devoured every word written about Cruise, but I'd put it down before finishing it, and I'm sure tens of thousands of other disheartened fans can relate. I love reading nonfiction books; whether they be about business icons, Hollywood stars and directors, and industries like television, the Internet, or media, I devour them.

But as I get older, I find myself shying away from celebrity books that are nothing but fluff. I don't want to read about who Frank Sinatra was rumored to sleep with (and there were many), nor do I care about what some one-time house maid thinks of Robert De Niro's relationship with his wife.

Yet there are hundreds of lame books of little or no credibility dealing with the world's biggest stars. And don't even get me started about books on the British Royals.

By the same token, I really don't want to read authorized biographies either, because they are usually nothing more than love notes to their subjects. Generally I find books written by newspaper or magazine reporters more interesting, because they are usually held up to the same journalistic standards that are evoked in their day jobs.

Usually.

TomKat

Tom Cruise and Katie Holmes had a daughter. They named her Suri. Welcome to civilization. Congratulations. Now go make a movie because that is all we care about. I will go see *M:I:III*. I won't be sending a onesie to your new daughter.

Brangelina

Interesting how with both couples, there's only one good actor, or box-office draw. As critic Kyle Smith of the *New York Post* put it, Tom Cruise is still "the world's best popcorn salesman." Meanwhile, has Katie Holmes made a movie anybody cared about?

Brad Pitt is a marginal actor at best. Jolie has the acting chops in that relationship.

Gay Grrr! Guy Wins Pulitzer

With all the hype surrounding the gay cowboy flick Brokeback Mountain, *I've come to the conclusion that the only way for me to get noticed by the elite media is to be gay.*

So, I'm gay.

In addition (I originally wrote "on top of that" but thought better of it), I'm also a recovering crack addict and am wheelchair bound after a drug-and-alcohol-induced motorcycle crash that left me paralyzed from the waist down.

It's only a matter of time now before the Pulitzer Prize and The Webby's committee take notice of the "Grrr!" column and send me the award for my "insightful and inspirational pop-culture rants."

Plus, The Weinstein Company will offer me big bucks for my story so that it can be adapted into an arthouse movie by Angels in America *scribe Tony Kushner and directed by none other than "Angst" Lee.*

After all, who better to direct the story of an American para-plegic/closeted gay columnist with a frustrated but gorgeous wife and a strapping lover on the side than a filmmaker from Taiwan?

My agent told me that although Sam Mendes of American Beauty *fame was a close runner-up for the director gig, he refused to lower his fee to meet the Weinsteins' budget.*

Of course, Joaquin Phoenix will play me, and Reese Wither-spoon my tortured and sexually frustrated but extremely loyal wife who bathes me and feeds me every day. Surely she'll win an Oscar for the portrayal of a strong woman who understands that being gay is a tortuous calling that trumps her needs.

However, in the best supporting actor category, Brad Pitt is a shoo-in for playing my equally loyal yet equally frustrated gay lover. The critics will praise him for playing against type by kissing Phoenix full on the mouth. He'll do promotion for the film with An-gelina Jolie by his side just to remind folks that he is as straight as they come.

Phoenix will not even be nominated because he refuses to kiss up to the Academy, since he knows that Hollywood is such horse poo that even Paris Hilton gets roles.

The pitch to The Weinstein Company *was pretty simple: It's* My Left Foot *meets* Wild Things *meets* Shakespeare in Love *meets* Walk the Line—*the latter being a nod to Lee's inspired-yet-unoriginal casting of Phoenix and Witherspoon.*

But just when you thought that being gay, paralyzed, married to Reese Witherspoon, and openly seeing Brad Pitt was enough to gar-ner all the critical praise that Hollywood and The New York Times *and* Ebert *and* Roeper *could offer, there's a twist.*

I also shot a man in Reno, just to watch him die.

Now I'm scheduled to be executed by lethal injection. This will of course bring on the Nobel Peace Prize committee, since my "insight-ful and inspirational column" is surefire proof that I am completely rehabilitated and have atoned for my crime, sparking a nationwide debate on the death penalty.

From death row I write about my visits from Dead Man Walking *star Susan Sarandon—who only used me for inspiration for her sympathetic nun character, by the way. But I was happy to oblige, although I would have liked a little "Special Thanks To" credit at the end of the film, but oh well.*

"Bitter, table for one."

Speaking of bitter, Graydon Carter from Vanity Fair *said my column stinks, but what does he know anyway? He kisses more butts than I do, and he's straight! But I digress.*

In case you're wondering, here's how the story ends.

I get clemency and am released from prison. Witherspoon refuses to leave my side and grows old with me, but Pitt leaves me for someone who not only can walk, but can carry off a cowboy hat—someone like Jon Voight in Midnight Cowboy, *and he figured he should keep it all in the family—and since Jolie kissed her brother full on the mouth at the Academy Awards a few years ago, it's all good with her.*

I get my own daytime talk show with Omarosa Maniqualt-Stallworth from The Apprentice's *first season as my sidekick, and together we are lauded by the critics and dethrone Oprah Winfrey from daytime's elite talk-show shelf.*

The Hollywood Foreign Press Association honors me by asking me to host the Golden Globes, where Jack Nicholson—after a few drinks—kisses me on the cheek and grabs my butt as he grins Joker-style at the star-studded crowd who can barely stay in their chairs, they're laughing so hard.

That Jack is just too cool.

Vanity Fair *invites me to their famed Oscar after-party and editor-in-chief Graydon Carter apologizes to me—publicly, mind you—making me the toast of Hollywood.*

Oh, and thanks to DuPont, I get artificial legs that help me play

*myself before the motorcycle crash in a CBS-TV miniseries based on
the "Angst" Lee movie about me.*

Thanks, America!

I wrote that column during the winter of 2005, when all the newspaper critics were saying that *Brokeback Mountain* was a sure best picture Oscar winner. *Crash* won, but *Brokeback* director Ang Lee did get
best director honors.

Whether I was right or wrong about how the elite media takes to
pet causes, like homosexual cowboys living heterosexual lies (imagine
a film about straight men cheating on their wives with young coeds being celebrated as much as *Brokeback Mountain* was), I still got plenty of
hate mail from people who took offense because of how they perceived the column.

What gets me is that anyone, gay or straight, who reads it with an
open mind might actually see that I was not even bashing gays. The column was meant to simply point out the absurdity of Hollywood and the
so-called "elite media" for their infatuation with anything and everything that pokes holes in anything that speaks "traditional," as in the
"tax-paying, career-driven, still-married, heterosexual couple not on drugs
raising healthy children" lifestyles that the majority of this country has.

That is *not* to say that homosexuals can't be all of the above. It's not
about homosexuals. It's about Hollywood.

Now, as an actor, I can understand the challenges Heath Ledger and
Jake Gyllenhaal faced in portraying closeted gay cowboys, both as artists
and as movie stars. Playing so against one's own type is both risky and
draining, but kissing a man on the lips in this homophobic society is
more risky and could be a career killer, so my hat is off to those guys.

However, the romanticizing of the film by the big-time media is just
so transparent. Amidst all of the hullabaloo and Oscar nominations
and fawning reviews, there was not one mention of the devastation such
a real-life sexuality crisis portrayed in the movie would cause a wife or

children. There was no talk of cheating on one's spouse with a lover, gay or straight. Why is that? The answer is simple. Homosexuality, according to the condescending liberals that run most of the media and Hollywood, is a torturous calling made worse by our homophobic society.

Bull-dinky.

Ask any homosexual how they would feel if their partner, whom they shared their home with, their finances with, raised a family with, and gave their everlasting love to, would feel if he left him for a woman. Do you think he'd be okay with it because "hey, he was straight, he must have been so conflicted"? Do you think that a movie made on that basis would have the same effect on the critics? Hell no.

What makes this country great is having the ability to live as one pleases, within the parameters of the law. I think that if someone is gay then so be it, as long as that someone respects the fact that I'm not, just as much as they want to be respected for their choices.

None of my gay friends believe that they deserve special treatment because they are gay. None. Just like none of my ethnic friends believe that they deserve special treatment because their skin is darker than someone else's. Heck, my skin is darker than most people's, and I don't walk around with a chip on my shoulder because my boss has lighter skin than me.

WHEN GOOD PRESS GOES BAD

So what happens when good press goes bad? What happens when a star or, in the case below, a couple of stars get so much exposure that eventually they become targets of hate columns by the same publications that propped them up in the first place?

Bennifer, anyone?

Not surprisingly, the much-maligned 2004 film *Gigli* tanked at the box office.

In its opening weekend, the $54 million Ben Affleck/Jennifer Lopez gangster romance took in less than $4 million. The film producers, who lost money, were disappointed, but probably not as much as Kevin Smith, the director of *Jersey Girl*, Affleck's and Lopez's next film together. These things happen.

However, judging from the torrent of venomous press that *Gigli* unleashed, one would think film critics and entertainment reporters were the ones who lost their shirts on this ill-fated project. Check out some of these quotes:

"Hopelessly misconceived exercise in celebrity self-worship, which opens to nationwide ridicule today."
—A. O. Scott, *The New York Times*

"Nearly as unwatchable as it is unpronounceable."
—Manohla Dargis, *Los Angeles Times*

"Every generation get the celebrities they deserve, but what have we done to deserve *Gigli*?"
—Duane Dudek, *Milwaukee Journal Sentinel*

"Witless, coarse and vulgar."
—Roger Friedman, foxnews.com

And believe me, those were not the worst. I won't even get into what the bloggers said. So what did Jen and Ben do to deserve such bad press? Brace yourselves: they made a bad movie.

Puhleez! High School anyone?

Imagine if the most popular couple in high school—the king and queen of the prom—tripped and fell flat on their faces while accepting their crowns. What would you do? Even though you voted for them, you'd probably laugh your butt off.

Essentially that's what happened to the former power couple. The press giveth, and the press taketh away.

During the "Bennifer" heyday, Affleck and Lopez graced countless magazine covers, were featured in segments on every entertainment show and were daily fodder for gossip columns.

Their interview with Pat O'Brien, which aired on a *Dateline NBC* special, earned super ratings, putting the show in the Nielsen's top ten for that week.

So they were overexposed. Big deal. If not them, it would be somebody else (Brad Pitt and Jennifer Aniston), and then somebody else (Brad Pitt and Angelina Jolie), and then somebody else (Jessica Simpson and Nick Lachey).

It bears reminding that Ben Affleck was an actor who had only modest success with commercials and a PBS series in a career that started when he was eight years old. After several unmemorable roles, *(School Ties, Chasing Amy)* he and childhood friend Matt Damon wrote *Good Will Hunting*—and the rest, as they say, is history.

But even that wasn't so simple. The actors' agent shopped the eventual-Oscar-winning script around to several studios before finally finding a home at indie-friendly Miramax.

Jennifer Lopez had it a little tougher. Growing up in the Bronx, one of New York City's tougher boroughs, little Jenny from the block used to take the subway into Manhattan for dance classes. After several years pounding the pavement, she got small parts in music videos and eventually landed a role as a Fly Girl on FOX's *In Living Color,* which starred the Wayans family and Jim Carrey, among others.

Lopez spent several more years in Hollywood before hitting it big playing Selena, the Latin pop star who was murdered by the president of her fan club.

Lopez's exposure to the music industry from that role and her earlier videos probably fueled the desire to become a pop star herself, which she eventually did to huge success, if not critical acclaim. She did earn critical accolades for her work with actor George Clooney in the noir film *Out Of Sight,* however (which also featured two of my favorite actors, Dennis Farina and Michael Keaton).

The point is, while sitting on top of the world these days, Affleck and Lopez were just two kids with dreams not too many years ago. Like most other hardworking Americans, they achieved success the old-fashioned way. They earned it. Or at least that's what their publicists tell us.

So why so bitter after one colossal failure?

"We really don't get anything from movie stars except entertainment," says psychologist Dr. Georgia Witkin, who runs the psych department at Mt. Sinai Hospital in Manhattan and has consulted actors to help them get into character. "Fans like them because they are beautiful and rich and we would love to trade places with them, but if they fail to entertain us, like in the case of *Gigli,* than what use do we have for them?"

Public relations consultant Ken Sunshine, a well-respected operator who has repped stars like Ben Affleck and Leonardo DiCaprio, among several others, says he can't prepare any of his clients for the inevitable onslaught of bad press.

"We have a sign in our office that says, 'The press is always right,'" said Sunshine. "The media will do what they're going to do. Celebrities can't obsess about what's written or said because if they do they'll go crazy, and they'll have a very short career."

BOLD-FACED NAMES

Don't you just love those columns from columnists who have nothing to say, except to sprinkle bold-faced names throughout their column? Wouldn't it be better if they were honest, and wrote something like this:

Tom Cruise has nothing to do with this column.

Except that **Tom Cruise** is in boldface.

And despite the controversy about the *South Park* episode **"Trapped** in the Closet" and the resulting war between the show's creators, Matt Stone and Trey Parker, and **Scientology** (or at least Cruise's lawyers), this column doesn't deal with it.

Tom Cruise is a nonissue to me.

Just as **John Travolta** and **Nicole Kidman** are also nonissues in this column.

But I did run into **Jamie-Lynn Sigler** at the **Mondrian Hotel** in Hollywood the Friday before the **Academy Awards.** The *Sopranos* beauty was in town filming an episode of something, and I was waiting for my car to come out of the valet after shooting a piece on the **Oscar "Preferred" Goodie Bag.**

The Oscar "preferred" goodie bag is just a misnomer, by the way, to get reporters like me to think that the person we're interviewing actually has something to do with the **Oscars,** when in fact they just represent a bunch of boutique firms that want to give free stuff to Oscar nominees with the provision that said nominees' names could be used in future marketing material.

"A massage bed used by **Matt Dillon,**" for instance.

Anyway, since I was standing around with a camera in tow, I asked Jamie-Lynn, who is more beautiful in person than she is on **HBO,** if she wanted to do a quick interview. Yes, I was joking, and she laughed appropriately.

Jamie-Lynn Sigler has a sense of humor.

But hey, I'm just putting her in the column because I can bold-face her name and thus attract your attention. In fact, I haven't said much of anything about any of the bold-faced names so far in the column.

But that's okay. It's customary for columnists to drop names, places, and new names for cocktails at "exclusive" bars in their columns.

After all, we have access, and you don't. Ha Ha Ha. How do you like that, "Grrr!" readers? I can go to a cooler-than-you party because I'm cooler than you. Ha!

Take that!

Never mind the fact that once in a room with so many other cool people, most reasonably sane people quickly realize that it's going to be really hard to write about this party and make it seem cool because it really isn't that cool.

I mean, I know **Patrick McMullen,** the celebrity photographer of *Kiss Kiss* fame, is running around with his camera, but I'm hard-pressed to find anybody really cool to talk about.

I know that **Dennis Hopper** is here and I know I'm supposed to think he's cool, but I never did get *Blue Velvet* and it's been a while since I recited the Sicilian/Moors monologue from *True Romance,* for obvious reasons.

But hey, I had a free Mojito, one of those ultra-cool beverages that is the specialty of the house at **The Ivy** in Santa Monica, a frequent haunt of **Lindsay (it's not Lo-Han it's Lowen) Lohan.**

That being said, "FOX 411" columnist **Roger Friedman** introduced me to the Beverly Hills power lunch spot **The Grille** on Dayton Way, where I conducted my Oscars gossip interviews.

The Grille was a very cool place, steeped in Hollywood history.

Of course, nothing all that scandalous happens there. For that you have to go to nightclubs like Butter or Bungalow 8 in New York, or for that matter **Rick's Cabaret,** the New York, Houston and Minneapolis mammary mecca chock-full of bold-faced names. Although Rick's is more discreet than say, Scores, in revealing its better-known clientele.

In Los Angeles, Skybar, Privilege, and Starbucks are also good for celeb sightings and anonymous call-ins to tabloid columns from tipsters, some of whom don't know that the term *canoodling* doesn't mean walking arm-in-arm; in fact, it's Page Six slang for making out.

Of course, it's a testament to pop culture that in this column full of bold-faced items, that city **Paris** and the **Hilton** hotel chain never once meet in successive letters.

Ah, how we've Grrrrrown . . . and no, I don't think I'm cooler than you. That's the joke.

A Reading From a Letter from
Mike to the Oblivions

Dear Oblivion Council:

I'm writing because I still haven't received my official Oblivion pin.

I have followed all of the rules set out in the brochure you sent me, which I received Nov. 2, and stayed in all day reading and plotting out my Oblivionism. What was I supposed to do on Nov. 2? Oh yeah, Election Day. Oh well, my vote probably wasn't important, anyway.

Anyway, I've been diligent in not writing my check at the grocery store until all of my goods have been rung up and bagged, and then I make sure my checkbook is all the way at the bottom of my bag. I even have this great thing where I pick several goods that have no price or barcode on them, so the clerk has to call for multiple price checks. It's the greatest.

I've also been good at ignoring all the instruction signs everywhere I go, so I have to ask someone in authority where or what I should do, much to their chagrin. To that point, I ask the same Starbucks clerk day in and day out what my cup size choices are, and then I say that I ordered decaf when the latte lady calls out my order. It's the coolest.

At the office, I tend to repeat what was just said by my colleagues and make it sound like it was my idea. I also like to let everybody know just how hard I work and how many long hours I put in. They call me The Martyr behind my back,

Grrr!

Continued

but I really don't mind. As long as my boss knows that I work harder than everybody else (despite the fact that if I did my job right in the first place, I wouldn't have to work so much longer than everybody else), I'll be okay.

Luckily for me, my boss is a bozo and can't see that I'm an idiot. It's the awesomest.

Will you please rush my Oblivion pin? I am enclosing a self-addressed stamped envelope for rush delivery. In fact, I'm standing at the U.S. Post Office counter right now, finishing this letter and addressing the envelopes while everybody else waits behind me, muttering under their breaths.

Wow, non-Oblivions are so nice. They put up with so much. No wonder they're way back there in line. It's just the peachiest.

Sincerely,

Mr. I. M. Oblivious

The Adventures of Johnny Oblivion and Suzie Wal-Martian

Johnny Oblivion wakes up in his fourth floor, paper-thin-walled apartment and blasts MTV so that his neighbors can enjoy *Video Wakeup* as he takes his morning shower. He leaves the TV on all day so his barking dog won't be lonely.

On his way to work he stops at the Dunkin' Donuts drive-thru and orders a cup of coffee. Despite the line of cars behind him, he sits at the window and puts sugar in his cup, tastes it, adds more sugar and tastes it again before putting the top back on and driving away.

On the road he weaves in and out of traffic in his Hummer H2 as he juggles the hot coffee in one hand and his cell phone in the other. He has to call his buddy and go over each inning of last night's darts baseball game at the local pub, where he also used some of his best pickup lines on the local ladies, like: "What are your plans for sex tonight?" (with credit to Bruce Willis, of course) and "You must know karate 'cause your body's kickin'."

As he travels 90 mph he notices a cop car has set up a radar trap ahead, so he slams on his brakes, nearly causing a pileup behind him.

When he arrives at his office, he parks in a spot reserved for someone else, sets his auto alarm, and enters his place of work. Of course, all his coworkers are soooo happy to see him, so he makes the rounds telling the men and women in the office about the babe he hooked up with the night before (not) and tops off his coffee with the last of the company brew without starting a fresh pot.

He sits in his cubicle and whistles loudly as he waits for his computer to boot up. Being extra-computer-savvy, he has rigged his PC to play Howard Dean's scream every time he gets a new e-mail, forcing his coworkers to relive that bit of Democratic agony all day long.

Johnny O. then punches the speaker button on his phone and listens to the dial tone as he tries to remember the voice mail number. He then checks his messages on speaker, commenting out loud on each and every call. One time a coworker of his posed as an angry client and berated him with curses and insults. The speaker phone was silent for about a day, so at least it worked for a few hours after that.

At lunch Johnny Oblivion orders Chinese food, which he eats at his desk, stinking up the entire office.

After work he hits the gym, where he rests on the bench press in between sets of leg exercises. He never notices the people waiting to use the bench press, and he never wipes his sweat off the bench when he gets up to resume his sets.

When he gets home, he walks his dog without a leash and lets it poop wherever it pleases. He won't pick up after his dog because he thinks littering creates jobs for sanitation workers.

He blasts Leno and laughs heartily into the wee hours of the night. When he finally goes to sleep, he dreams of the time he belly-flopped repeatedly in the public pool, and wonders why the mothers of the young children give him dirty looks whenever he arrives.

Because . . . He . . . Is . . . An . . . Oblivion.

Johnny O. is a one-upper in the Susan Wal-Martian fashion, except he's the sports, investing, and women expert. Whenever the subject of any sport comes along, he was All-State Everything back in his day, and each conversation usually ends with a demonstration of clapping push-ups, even in the office.

Every Monday night after *The Ultimate Fighter* on Spike TV, Johnny goes running and kicks the oak tree out in his backyard to condition his shins, just in case he finds himself with an opportunity to step into the Octagon.

And heaven forbid he catches you eyeing a stock quote, because he's got the best investment strategy this side of Warren Buffett. Monkey index, anyone?

But women are Johnny Oblivion's bread and butter.

He knows exactly how to pick up women, and more important, he knows how to turn them on. For instance, while seated across from his date at a fancy restaurant, Johnny O. likes to slowly bring his food up to his mouth, and he savors each bite while looking longingly into the eyes of his would-be paramour.

He hasn't quite mastered the art of eating quietly, however. He munches and mashes his food like a pig eating slop left over from the night before.

Johnny Oblivion's driveway looks like a body shop, but he actually has a very nice lawn. Every weekend he's out there bright and early with the weed whacker, meticulously edging and trimming. He's even got a fence to keep the neighborhood canines at bay.

Johnny Oblivion is famous for his bad driving. Cops know him because he always chirps his tires when he pulls away from a red light, he tailgates everybody, and he takes turns at about 20 mph faster than he should.

Johnny is also an ImporTant. He loves to talk on his cell phone with imaginary underlings, making believe he's berating someone for a job poorly done, and when his phone actually rings in the middle of his tirade, he actually tells the nonexistent person on the other end to hold on while he takes another call.

He must have the only cell phone that rings externally when there's a call waiting.

Johnny Oblivion is a know-it-all to the umpteenth degree. He knows more about politics than Bill O'Reilly, he's got more athletic ability in his pinky than Michael Jordan has in his entire body, and he knows more about movies than Leonard Maltin.

He does all his own electrical and plumbing work in his house, making Rube Goldberg look like Albert Einstein.

Like Suzie Wal-Martian, we all know someone like Johnny Oblivion. And we all indulge him in our own way.

MEET SUZIE WAL-MARTIAN

When it comes to annoying the average citizen, Suzie Wal-Martian takes the cake.

Suzie is delighted to see her next-door neighbors among the cereals, whom she doesn't deign to speak with at home, but she'll block the entire aisle with her cart to blab endlessly with them, catching up on the last five years and the latest deaths in the neighborhood.

Never mind the people sighing loudly as they maneuver by her. She doesn't even notice.

Of course, she pushes her cart into the nearest empty parking space after loading her goods into her Hummer (with the rear light guards, of course, because you never know when the brush at the local Starbucks will get overgrown). Of the cart she tells her bridge-playing buddies, "Somebody gets paid to round up those carts. It's not my job."

After leaving the store, Suzie has a problem merging onto the highway with such a large vehicle, so she sits at the yield sign and waits until there is absolutely no traffic in the right lane, wondering why people behind her are leaning on their horns.

When Suzie Wal-Martian is hungry she likes to go to Subway for the low-fat sandwiches. (Incidentally, a note to Subway: lose Jared.) Anyway, Suzie goes to Subway practically every day during her lunch break. But no matter how many times she's been there, the concept of knowing what she wants when she gets to the front of the line is way too much for her. No matter how long she's been waiting to order, she still has to ponder the merits of the plain Italian roll versus the Parmesan cheese alternative.

At her favorite restaurant, it's very important for Suzie to let her waiter or waitress know that she is a regular customer, so she'll give them a review of exactly what was wrong with her last meal there, then order the exact same thing. Tip? Five percent is plenty.

In the morning, Suzie is very keen on smelling good, so right before she gets out of her car she sprays a considerable amount of her White Diamonds perfume all over herself, so she's smelling of powdery flowers for the packed elevator ride up to her office. "You never know who'll take notice." Or who might actually be allergic!

When several people sneeze she turns and blesses them, commenting on just how bad allergy season is this year.

Suzie Wal-Martian embodies everything that is annoying in an Oblivion.

At the office she's everybody's big sister, making sure coworkers are getting to the doctor to get that persistent cough checked out, or commenting on the attire of everyone within sight, always drawing attention to people who don't necessarily care for it.

"Wow, that's a terrific sweater Janeane. Great tie, Joe."

But perhaps Suzie's most annoying quirk is how every story anybody is telling always seems to relate to Suzie. It's magical, really.

For instance, if someone has a headache, well, Suzie has migraines that debilitate her whenever they come on. In fact, she usually keeps a bottle of green apple shampoo that she can sniff whenever she feels a migraine coming on, but when asked to produce said bottle says she must have left it at home.

When Suzie has a rash on her back it's actually a case of shingles, and the pain in her shoulder is most definitely bursitis or early onset arthritis, something that just happens to run in her family.

And please don't bring up any bathroom ailments, because she will top you with irritable bowel syndrome or two weeks' worth of painful constipation. This time she can produce the extralarge package of Ex-Lax that brings me back to my wrestling days where I would try anything to cut weight.

Whenever a television segment that deals with health comes along, people who know Suzie, like family or friends, try desperately to change the channel lest they get stuck listening to how the latest medical discovery will change her life in some way, shape, or form.

When Suzie is actually sick and needs tests, she'll tell people that "they" are sending her for tests or "they" are sending her for an MRI, as if she is a special case that has the medical community collectively baffled and intrigued. *"They* are sending me for X-rays."

Wow, Suzie, and to think that my personal physician ordered X-rays for me just last week. I had no idea that X-rays were so mysterious. I guess I should have been more worried about the procedure.

Of course, hypochondria isn't the only annoyance that Suzie Wal-Martian has mastered. Don't forget that when anchorman Peter Jennings died, he was her "favorite newsman," even though her television is locked on a channel that is not ABC, not to mention that she hasn't watched the evening news in decades.

And besides, we all thought the late David Bloom was her favorite newsman. At least that's what she said when he died.

Of course her favorite television show was *Arrested Development*, which was "tragically cancelled," but she doesn't know who played Bob Loblaw.

Any and all discussions somehow always come back to Suzie. When she was a kid, nobody talked back to adults, and if she did, her mother or father would "smack me upside the head." Of course, when a conversation about abusive parents come up, her parents "wouldn't think of hitting me."

She is the ultimate Polignorant [see GRRR! Lexicon] who complains about whatever administration happens to occupy the White

House but who never gets to the voting booth because she is simply too busy. But she'll vote next time for sure.

She's the type of person who will adopt the opinion of whichever authority she happened to read or catch on the cable channel as her own, not really knowing where she stands. All she knows is that it sounded good when she heard it.

In short, we all know someone like Suzie Wal-Martian, and we all indulge her by being a *good friend,* and good listeners.

Then we talk about her.

(((13)))

Grrrs Gone Wild and Other Random Events That Will Drive You Crazy

SLURP, SLURP, SLURP

GRRRRRRRRRRRRRRR!

That's how I felt riding an elevator with an Oblivion coffee slurper, some guy whose coffee was obviously too hot to drink normally.

So instead of waiting for the darn cup to cool off, he took baby slurps. *Slurrrrrrp . . . slurrrrrrrp.* Oh, the sound of that slurping made me want to grab that cup of coffee and pour it over his head.

Don't you just hate the sound of people and their food?

I'm no Mr. Manners, that's for sure, but I do not eat, drink, or chew gum with my mouth open, smacking my lips and gums to the tune of "My Darling Clementine." Whatever happened to basic table manners anyway?

It's not like we can blame Bart Simpson for the lack of table etiquette. Can't blame MTV. Can't even blame Paris Hilton, and when you can't blame Paris Hilton for something that makes you go Grrrr! then you know we've got a real issue to deal with.

So what is it about loud eaters? Did their parents never explain proper eating etiquette to them because they themselves were Oblivions in their child rearing? Perhaps the loud eater is an only child whose parents never, ever disciplined them for anything.

But what about the loud eaters' adult spouses or significant others? Are they that insecure that they can't point out to the offending eater just how disgusting their eating habits are? "Wouldn't want to offend my honey."

Puhleez!

Oblivions need to close their mouths. It's really not that hard, unless you have rotten teeth.

Another thing that gets my goat are hard swallowers. These are people who seemingly collect their beverage at the top of their throats and swallow it down all at once, making a loud gulp.

Are they exercising their peristalsis muscles in their throats?

My older brother used to make me Grrr! every single morning at breakfast. Even when I was in grade school, the sound of eating made my skin crawl, so my brother would pucker his lips while eating his Cheerios.

Imagine the sound of crunchy cereal, milk, and *puck-puck-puck.* It's disgusting.

Another thing that drives me up a wall is when people don't use napkins when they eat. Instead, they lick their fingers, pucking up after each lick. Buffalo wing eaters are the worst offenders.

I once pointed out to a fellow diner that he had food on his cheek. Do you think he'd grab a napkin and wipe it off? Well, most people would, but since he happened to be at *my* table, and these things tend to drive me crazy, he sticks his tongue out and tries to lick it off his cheek.

There he was, at dinner, slithering his tongue like a snake, stretching it to reach the food. Did I mention that his tongue was still covered in food?

Are you that hungry that you can't just wipe your face with a napkin?

Are you that lazy that you'd rather lick the hot sauce off your fingers instead of using a napkin? Were your parents wolves?

Food Etiquette

Lack of food etiquette is a surefire sign of Oblivionism, and it usually stems back to one's childhood when Mom or Dad never bothered to explain—or failed to demonstrate—the proper way to eat one's food. Here are a few pointers for the mandible-challenged.

o **Smacking Your Food Is Bad.** It's not very pleasant when people can hear you chewing food, unless you're munching on Doritos. Please try to close your mouth while chewing.

o **Don't Talk with Your Mouth Full.** Talking at the dinner table is a wonderful thing, but why wait until your mouth is full to make your point? This is simple, folks. When you put food in your mouth, don't speak until your mouth is empty.

o **Gulp Gulp Gulp.** Unless you've got blockage of the esophagus, liquid should flow down your throat quietly. Peristalsis is a wonderful thing, but you don't need to prove how tough your esophageal muscles are with each gulp.

o **Don't Touch My Food.** I have a food thing: if you touch mine, you can finish it, because I won't want any of it after you've put your hands, mouth, or used utensil on it. Just ask, and I'll be happy to cut you a piece with my knife, then slide it off my plate onto yours. I don't need any help getting it to you.

Grrr!

Continued

○ **Mind Your Own Business.** Just because you can smell a coworker's french fries as you walk by their cubicle doesn't mean that's an open invitation to comment on what they're eating. "I didn't know you ate that! That's not good for you." And what the hell does that have to do with you? I must have missed the memo where everybody had to eat the same thing every day.

VOICE MAIL: CAN IT TAKE ANY LONGER TO GET TO THE BEEP?

Voice-mail options are getting a little ridiculous, don't you think?

It's the twenty-first century, for crying out loud. Is there anyone out there who doesn't know that they should wait for the tone before leaving a voice-mail message?

It's one thing when you get someone's voice mail, and you hear his voice saying something like, "Hi, you've reached the voice mail of Joe Oblivion. Sorry I can't take your call right now, but leave me a message after the beep." That's a perfect outgoing message—short and sweet. But then an automated voice comes on with all kinds of instructions: "To leave a callback number. . . . press five. Otherwise, leave your message at the tone. . . . Record at the tone. . . . After you are done recording, press pound for more options."

More options? At that point the only option I'm interested in is: "To zap the person you are trying to reach with a few amps of electricity, press the star key."

Are we supposed to be impressed by the multitude of options on your cell service? Do people need so many options? Seriously!

THE IMPORTANT ON SPEAKER PHONE

Hey, ImporTant, look around you. See those cubicles around you? See those people working hard, concentrating on getting their jobs done? Those are your coworkers, and believe it or not, they don't care to listen in on your phone conversations or your voice-mail messages.

So please save them the daily Grrr! and order yourself a headset, or pick up the darn handset and put it to your ear. Are you that lazy? Are you that concerned that your boss or your coworkers know how hard you work?

Here's a news flash for you: if you don't have an office door to close— so you can use your speakerphone without disturbing everybody— you're not that ImporTant.

But if your coworker insists on letting everyone in on their speaker-phone messages, have a buddy make a crank call to their voice mail, posing as some unhappy high-level client, and leave a message ripping him a new one. Or, you can have someone call from the local gay club and announce that he left his credit card at the bar.

Eventually he'll get the picture. If nothing else, the rest of the office will get some free entertainment.

OBLIVIONS-IN-TRAINING

No matter where you go, the Oblivions will follow.

For example, coming back East from a trip to Los Angeles one weekend, I was treated to a father, a son, and a daughter who boarded the rental car shuttle for the Midwest Air terminal.

While the kids slung their bags over their shoulders and nearly broke the nose of the person behind them—without acknowledging the gaffe, mind you—the father was busy balancing a Sausage McMuffin and a cup of coffee in one hand and his cell phone in the other, all the while carrying on a conversation that was apparently hilarious, because he laughed heartily and loudly the whole ride.

When we came to the Midwest Air terminal, the family never got up, despite two announcements from the driver. Finally, after the driver walked up to them to ask them if they were getting off, they all sprang up from their seats, awakened out of their Oblivion trance.

The son stepped on the toes of an elderly woman who yelped in pain. He never apologized.

The daughter said "Duh," so at least she acknowledged her brother's Oblivionism. But the father—now he was a study in Oblivionism—never got off the phone as the kids got their own bags and wreaked their own havoc. He continued to wolf down his breakfast while—get this—the driver unloaded his bags for him.

Dad never said thank you.

Needless to say, when the doors closed and we proceeded to the next terminal, the entire shuttle bus released a huge sigh of relief.

That, my friends, is a true Oblivion encounter. Even worse, Daddy Oblivion is training his children to behave as abhorrently as he does. I've said it before: it's amazing that in this great nation one needs a license to drive a car, a boat, and a motorcycle; we are required by law to wear seat belts and helmets and to not smoke in public establishments—but *anyone* can have a child. Anytime. Grrr!

And speaking of Oblivion parents:

I was burning mad over a quote I saw in a local newspaper in a story about the tragic choking death of a five-year-old boy.

His mother told reporters that her child was blowing up a latex rubber glove like a balloon—and said she yelled at him to stop. Even though the boy didn't listen, the woman made no effort to actually get up and take the glove from him. A few moments later a piece of the glove lodged in the boy's throat and he died.

Beside the obvious, tragic Grrr! the woman actually went on to say that her child died "because the paramedics took too long to get there." Huh?

Apparently, the ambulance took twenty minutes to arrive on the scene. My question: How long would it have taken for Mom to get up off her lazy @$&! and take the dangerous toy away from her toddler son? This was a tragedy that could have been avoided.

Wake up, parents, and start parenting. Or is the life of your child something that can be replaced by a lawsuit against an ambulance company or a wealthy city?

LIP MUMBLING

Why do people take it upon themselves to sing songs to which they do not know the words? You ever notice people mouthing the wrong words to songs that are playing on the jukebox or the radio?

I call it "Lip Mumbling."

Do you think we don't notice? Or better yet, do you think we think you're cool even if you did know the words? When I was a kid I used to think "Paperback Writer" by the Beatles was really "Take the Back Right Turn." Try singing it like that the next time you hear it. It makes me laugh every time I hear the song. But I was ten years old!

And don't you just cringe when some popular singer misses his opening line when he is supposedly performing live on television? I used to get so angry about catching singers lip-synching during live appearances, but nowadays I just change the channel. Oh, and I don't buy their CDs.

And how about people who say "seen" when they really mean to say "saw"? "I seen him yesterday." What? To make matters worse, I know a guy who says "sawl" instead of "saw." "I sawl her yesterday," or, "I sawled the two-by-four in half." Sawl!

By the way, people try *to* do something; they don't try *and* do something.

And why do famous, overpaid athletes always answer questions directed at them by referring to themselves as *you*? For example:

Reporter: "Are you looking forward to playing for a winning team?"

Overpaid Athlete: "Well, you come out to the field and you do the best you can, and hopefully you win."

What, is the reporter all of a sudden a teammate?

"COULD CARE LESS"

"I could care less." Now there's a phrase that is not only overused, it's wrong.

When you "could care less," you actually care enough about something that you could manage to care a few degrees less about it. Are you following me? Most people who say this (like a lot of you who send me hate e-mail about the GRRR! column) really mean to say, "I *couldn't* care less."

Please, when sending me hate mail, try to use proper English. It dilutes and discredits your otherwise feel-good notes. Strakalogue@ foxnews.com.

TECHNICAL "SUPPORT"

In a lot of cases, *tech support* is an oxymoron. When my high-speed DSL line was not working, yet again, I called technical support, and all I got was some help-line employee looking to get me off the phone.

"Do you have a speaker near your modem? Do you have a cordless phone? Do you know if you have a security system?"

Do I know if I have a security system? I should hope I know! Do you mean to ask me if I have a security system, or if I simply know if I have one?

After unplugging every phone in the house and isolating the modem, the problem still persisted, prompting the help expert to determine the problem must be the alarm, never mind the fact that I had this problem before I even had an alarm.

Explain that, oh help-line operator.

Actually, don't bother. The next call I made was to the cable company. Not only did I order a cable modem for my Internet access, I also switched to voice-over IP for my phone service, thereby eliminating my need to ever contact the phone company for anything ever again. In fact, I cut the telephone wire from my home and sealed the hole in my siding. No more bells for me, ever.

ON THE FLIP SIDE

But let's not forget that these technical support employees are subjected to more Oblivion behavior in one day than most of us see in a month.

So, let's remember to turn our computers on before calling the help line. Don't wait until you're in the car to call technical support on your cell phone about problems on your home PC or its Internet connection. It won't help the technician troubleshoot your problem if you're not sitting in front of your computer.

And when you're dealing with a tech support worker who really knows tech, it's useless to try to fool her. Therefore, if you did hit that delete button, or if you did download that virus, just tell the truth. It will save a lot of time for both you and them. And if you are looking at the software window and you can't see the giant "to get started" button on the screen (because it was too obvious for you to see—it happens), don't act like it just appeared on your screen out of nowhere when you finally do see it, after yelling at the tech. They know better.

BEER COMMERCIALS

If aliens came down to earth, not only would they think dogs were the masters of the planet, but if they catch a beer commercial or two, they'd think all men are morons.

We scream at the top of our lungs as we raise our frosty mugs in unison.

We ogle silicone babes who wouldn't notice us anyway because they're way too busy looking at themselves, or wondering which VH 1 or E! special they'll be appearing on as pop-culture "experts."

And what's with so many dorky, beer guzzling, pot-bellied, bad-mannered guys getting all the hot chicks in commercials? Yeah, that's realistic.

Advertising executives are laughing all the way to the bank.

And those actors! Having done several television commercials my-self, it Grrrs me probably more than even the most jaded viewers to see actors schticking it up in commercials. I can imagine every time certain spots air that there's an actor sitting on some couch with a group of friends explaining proudly how "that part where I lick my sweaty armpit was all my idea"—or something idiotic like that. I know actors have to take what they can get in hopes that something will get them noticed, but there's gotta be a better way than acting like a complete moron on national television. Then again, it does work for reality tele-vision stars.

CONGRATULATIONS! YOU'RE PREAPPROVED

My wife and I received an unsolicited preapproval letter for credit the other day from a large bank. The interest rate: 19.99 percent. Wooohoooo, sign us up baby! Yeah, right.

Whenever I get these preapproved offers with ridiculous APRs, I circle the interest rate (usually hard to find because of the fine print) and write "Get real" on it.

Then I send it back in the prepaid envelope.

I do this so the bank's employees can waste the same amount of their time opening what they think is an application—as I wasted opening the "great offer" letter.

DISINFECTANT WIPES

I'm a big fan of disinfectant wipes from Clorox, for instance, among others. However, I'm not a fan of the dispenser. When you get to the end of the container, the wipes aren't long enough to reach the opening on the cap, forcing one to pry open the top, which usually results in bleeding beneath a fingernail or something just as aggravating.

MY BABY IS GORGEOUS

We all think our babies are gorgeous. However, just because your uncle, neighbor, or sorority sister works in show business in some capacity, don't ask them to get your kid a talent agent.

It takes a lot more than having a cute baby to get them in commercials or movies, and most parents don't have the time, money, or energy for the (mostly failing) journey. Watch Bravo's frighteningly real documentary-style show *Showbiz Moms and Dads,* before you decide your kid is the next Life Cereal Mikey.

YOUR SCREENPLAY

The same goes for your screenplay or your idea for the next big reality show. If you believe in yourself, move to Los Angeles or New York, sacrifice your career, live life in a hovel, and commit to your craft. Eventually, you'll be able to get the break you need, but if you're not in it, you are not going to win it. Simply buying ScreenWriter software for your PC doesn't mean you're going to be the next William Goldman, and nobody you know is going to put themselves out there for you. Chances are, they worked their ass off to get what little success they have, so why would they just hand it to you without the work? They wouldn't. Would you?

WANNABE ACTORS

All you need is a headshot and a dream, right?

Actually, no. You need a great head shot that will cost you big bucks, you need great talent that you can achieve only by taking classes with great teachers that will cost you big bucks, you need to move to a city where there's theater, like New York or Los Angeles, and then you have to act in plays, which pays little, if any, and where the cost of living is astronomical, forcing you to work crazy hours, which means bartending or waiting on tables, which also means very little income, so now you're stuck in some town with no money, a business—because that's what acting is, folks—a business with little prospects for success and extreme competition for what few jobs are available, and the eternally elusive quest for an agent.

Next thing you know you're forty years old, still single, still renting, still no children, and still no talent. Wake up folks. Stardom is a commitment.

CLAMSHELL PACKAGING

Okay. After maneuvering the lumber-cart obstacle course at Home Depot and surviving the self-checkout line behind the Oblivion who is probably still there, you're finally home and ready to install that new dimmer switch you needed for the dining room light fixture.

But now there's a slight problem. When you go to install it you can't get the darn package open. Whose bright idea was clamshell packaging anyway? It's everywhere. Toys, computer hardware, tools, and countless other products are so hard to open you'll need to buy a pair of heavy-duty scissors to get to them.

Is crime that big a problem? Okay, fine, clamshell packaging may be necessary, but then when I purchase my dimmer switch, I should demand that a Home Depot representative open it for me with the proper tools.

COMMUTER OBLIVIONS

My commuter bus has a sign that reads, "As a courtesy to other passengers, please limit cell phone use to emergency calls only." Would be nice if people paid heed, but it would be even nicer if the bus driver didn't have his CB radio tuned *louder* than most Oblivions talk on their cell phones. All morning long today: *choook*—"Hey Bobby, what are you doing after the shift?"—*chook*—"Dispatch to twenty-two, what's your twenty-four?"—and on and on.

E-MAIL OBLIVIONS

Here's to all of the e-mail-challenged people out there:

When forwarding that chain letter or that stupid joke of the day that most of your recipients are deleting anyway, first copy the text into a new e-mail. Try this:

1. Highlight only the text of the joke or stupid chain letter you want to send by left clicking your mouse, and dragging the cursor to the end of the message. Now let go of the mouse. Hit the CTRL and C keys on your keyboard simultaneously.

2. Now, compose a new e-mail message as if you were sending a new e-mail.

3. Put the cursor in the message body of your blank e-mail and hit the CTRL and V keys on your keyboard simultaneously.

4. Now enter your desired recipient's e-mail address in the "To" field and enter a subject in the "Subject" field.

5. Click "Send."

Or better yet, don't. Our inboxes are cluttered enough with legitimate e-mail, spam, and so on. Do your friends a favor and just delete the chain e-mails.

BOOKS WITH LOTS OF PICTURES

I love reading nonfiction, particularly biographies.

But how hard would it be for the editors to end a chapter *before* putting in twenty pages of pictures and captions? By the time I go through all the pictures, I have to go back to pick up the midsentence where the pictures started because I forgot where the story was. Is this some kind of book editor's joke? Perhaps my editor at St. Martin's Press can add an editor's note here with an explanation. [Books are bound in signatures of thirty-two or sixteen pages each. The photo insert is put into the middle of the book after a signature. The midpoint signature does not often fall before a chapter beginning.]

WHAT GOES THROUGH THE MIND OF AN OFFICE OBLIVION

"Woe is me. I can't get ahead in life. But please, Mr. and Ms. Employer, don't ask me to put in any extra effort unless you pay me for it. I expect and deserve to be compensated for every minute of overtime! Gee, I wonder why I've been stuck in the same cubicle and with measly cost-of-living increases for the past however many years—and that sucker who gives this place his or her all and never complains gets the office and the promotion. Must be a kiss-ass. Yeah, that's the ticket. *I'll* never kiss butt. I've got my pride."

PET CAUSES

Much was made of Bravo's *Inside The Actor's Studio* interview with Jennifer Lopez. Apparently several Latin advocacy groups were upset because out of all the great Latin actresses out there, they didn't think J.Lo was worthy of being the first Latin actress on such a prestigious interview show.

Huh? It's a fluff show. Am I the only one sick and tired of the little pet causes that are anachronistic, to say the least? Host James Lipton will do his research, he'll flatter J.Lo with his grand knowledge of her work, and his audience will applaud her every answer. And, oh, by the way, it will rate higher than an interview with Chita Rivera, or any other so-called "important" Latina actress. Nothing against Ms. Rivera.

PETA

And how about PETA? The People for the Ethical Treatment of Animals started out having a good cause before becoming militant. Throwing paint on fur coats, as members are wont to do from time to time, does more harm than good. Insurance companies get stuck paying for replacement furs—driving up premiums for everybody—and more animals are killed in the coat replacement process.

Do they really think Anna Wintour won't go out and buy another fur coat?

ELEVATOR OBLIVIONS

You know, the elevator doesn't come any faster if you push the button multiple times. If you hold the "door close" button while ascending or descending, it will still stop on the floors it was called to. If the light is already lit, someone already pushed the button. In most cases, the "door open" and "door close" buttons are deactivated unless a fire warden turns the key on the panel.

THE BANK

In these technologically advanced days, when one can bank or buy and sell stocks online, why does it still take several days for a check to clear after it is deposited?

Restaurant Grrr!s That Will Make You Lose Your Appetite

Where do I begin? I'm a stickler for service.

I took the family to a Houlihan's restaurant. We were pleasantly surprised. The uniforms were crisp and clean . . . white shirt, black vest, and tie . . . and the service was really out of this world. I was shocked that this was a chain restaurant. Finally, people who care about and have pride in what they do!

However, that is not usually the case. How many times do you go into chain restaurants and get the "not a care in the world" host who asks, "Can I help you?" No, actually I just came in to check what song was playing on your too-*loud* speakers!

Ever go into a restaurant right after the lunch rush when the place is empty? The music is so loud it's impossible to hold a conversation. And what's with the '70s disco music in these places? Like I really need to hear "Love to Love You Baby" at three in the afternoon.

And what's with the bartenders these days who are too cool to start a conversation with their customers? Last week I was sent on assignment to Cleveland and had time to kill at the airport, so I stopped at a bar. I spent an hour nursing a brew and staring at a muted television screen. Fortunately, it was locked on FOX News Channel and I was able to read the crawl. Where was the bartender? She was having a conversation with two waitresses in the corner and barely looked up to see if

I, or anybody else for that matter, needed anything. Let me guess, was she complaining about bad tips? Hah!

But how about the customer who announces to his table what he is going to order? This irritates me to no end. He exclaims to his friends or business acquaintances, "I'm gonna have the teriyaki chicken salad!" Who cares? Tell the waiter. Or how about the people who begin the order with the words "let me get." "Let me get a Big Mac with a supersize Coke." What do you mean "let me get"? Are you going to go behind the counter and get it yourself?

WHAT GOES THROUGH THE MIND OF A DRIVE-THRU OBLIVION

Hmmm, what should I order off the drive-thru menu? Should I get a chicken sandwich or a burger? A salad or the chili? Coke or root beer? Should I supersize it? Oh, this is difficult.

"Ummm, hold on, I'm still looking. Okay? Okay? Is this thing on?"

Hmmm, where was I? Maybe I should check the wallet to see what kind of cash I have on hand before I decide.

"Hey, stop beeping at me. Jerk."

Twelve dollars, okay. I guess it'll be a number six. "I'll have a number six . . . thanks." *I'll pull up to the window, I guess.* "Thank you. Can I get some extra ketchup? And napkins." *Now I'm going to sit here and check that I got everything . . . ooh, darn.* "Hey, I said no cheese. There's cheese on this burger." *These people who work in the drive-thru are so stupid!*

"Don't beep at me. I said 'no cheese.' It's not my fault."

THE CHEAP STRAW

I don't know the history of fast-food paper products, but I will say that lately going to Mickey D's for a thick chocolate shake has become an exercise in futility. Why?

Well, the shakes themselves are still thick and delicious. They are not the problem. And for the most part, ordering simply a shake reduces your chance that some counter clerk will mix up your order with the dude who likes extra onions on his Big Mac. Yuck.

No, the problem I have with a thick, delicious McDonald's shake is that I can't enjoy it like I used to. At least not without bursting a blood vessel in my brain. And that's because the straws they dole out these days are made of such tiny plastic that the action of sucking on them to access the thick delicious shake causes the straw to collapse in on itself, thereby blocking the frosty beverage like the arterial sclerosis the French fries will give you anyway.

So there you are, sucking harder and harder, trying to get at the shake, and all the while the harder you suck, the harder it is for the shake to get through the straw. It's a comedy of errors if you think about it. So now you have no choice but to wait for the shake to melt down and be less thick, so that you can enjoy it, which begs the question; should McDonald's simply make their shakes less thick? Well, I would venture to say no, 'cause they are thick and delicious as is. What they need to do is have a soft-drink straw that can be paper for all anyone cares, and a shake straw that could be a version of PVC pipe for all anyone cares.

Just let me get to my shake, please.

DUNKIN' DONUTS

I love my neighborhood Dunkin' Donuts. The manager, Allen, regularly asks me about my family, and he and his staff know exactly what I want when I walk in.

But I've had my share of Oblivion moments inside Dunkin' Donuts.

Butter Please

I was in Dunkin' Donuts the other day, getting a caffeine fix (like I need any more stimulation). Anyway, some clown in front of me ordered a bagel with butter. The clerk put two pats of butter in the bagel bag, and the clown *flipped out.*

"You messing with me? Is that what you're doing? You messing with me?" he asked the clerk.

He then turned around, looking for approval from me. This is not the first time I've been in a DD line when someone had a beef with the clerk and they turned to me for some empathy, by the way. Seems like I'm an Obliviot magnet.

The guy looked at me and said, "I asked this guy for butter and this is what he gives me." I replied, "Sir, with all due respect, I couldn't care less if he put butter on your bagel or not. I'm here for a cup of coffee, not to ally with you or anybody else against the clerk."

Needless to say, he was he upset with me. He crumpled his wax paper bag and stormed off with his bagel and butter pats in tow. Classic Obliviot. The thing is, people don't like to be called out on their Oblivionism.

Look, nobody's perfect. In fact, I get my share of "you stink"

Random Annoyances

o Broadsheet newspapers, like *The New York Times* or *USA Today,* should offer tabloid-style versions of their papers for commuters to read on buses and trains. That commuter fold is waaay over my head.

o Why do people adopt the foreign or regional accent of the person with whom they are speaking? Please stop. Nothing worse than hearing that New Yawker start to sound just like the salesman from Texas or Britain.

o Why are there extra surcharges on parking or moving violation tickets? Just set the fines higher. I've always viewed parking tickets and a lot of moving violations as legal extortion anyway, so they might as well go for it.

o Why do people at concerts or ball games sit in empty seats that don't coincide with the ticket they purchased? There's nothing worse than going for a brew or to the restroom and returning to some Oblivion sitting in your seat. Happens all the time. These people should be brought out to the field and flogged.

o Why do suburban moms need Hummer H2s? Just because Hummer made them a little cheaper so you wouldn't have to be a highly paid movie star or an athlete to afford one doesn't mean you need one. Oh yeah, I know. Don't tell you what you do or don't need. I get it.

Grrr!

e-mails. And sometimes I *do* stink. The "Grrr!" column has had its moments of mediocrity, I admit that. But I can take the criticism.

Sadly, Oblivions can't see the error in their own ways (which makes them Oblivions), and instead of trying to correct their behavior, they blame us—the non-Oblivions—and march off on their not-so-merry ways.

(((15)))

Blame It on the Rain . . . or Purple Ink . . . or Anybody but Me . . .

PURPLE INK FAIRIES

We have parents who overprotect their little darlings and want to bequeath to them self-esteem.

Purple ink fairies, anyone?

Did you hear about this movement by some parents to remove red magic markers from schools because the red ink was too stressful to children?

So, they petitioned grade school teachers to trade in their red magic markers for purple ones when grading papers for their precious little entitled darlings.

After decades of using red ink, some teachers and psychologists are saying the ink's negative connotation is too harsh on students who pour their little hearts into their studies.

Yeah, right. What does that mean for the student whose A grade appears in red ink? Should that student cower in fear and never turn in an A paper again?

If you ask me, it's this type of thinking that's part of the problem. Stop coddling kids and help them take responsibility for their actions, or lack thereof. If they don't like red ink (gasp!), they should study harder.

It's as simple as that.

Stop looking for ways to make failing someone else's fault! Face it, parents, no matter how much you want your kid to be terrific, one cannot gain self-esteem other than by earning it oneself.

ULTIMATE FIGHTING AS ROLE MODEL?

Okay . . . so you're not a fan of Ultimate Fighting or mixed martial arts competitions. I can't say I blame you. Fighting is not for everyone.

But if you can get past the scariness of witnessing two athletes going toe-to-toe in the middle of a ring called "The Octagon," you might find a lesson worth passing on to your kids, or one for yourself.

On Spike TV's *The Ultimate Fighter*, a reality show that puts the word *real* back in reality television, an aspiring professional fighter named Sammy Morgan, a Minneapolis landscaper and nightclub security guard, stepped into the ring with one of the most talented and fierce fighters the reality show had ever seen, a completely unassuming guy named Luke Cummo.

Luke was pretty much a dork.

He meditated, ate the weirdest concoctions of food, and had a unique way of training. What everybody learned after seeing Luke fight is that what may look unconventional for some can be the secret to success for others.

Luke turned out to be the real deal.

When Sammy and Luke squared off, viewers and fight fans were treated to a round-one action reminiscent of the legendary bout between Forrest Griffin and Stephen Bonner from the show's legendary first season finale. Round two brought a different reality, however.

Luke knocked Sammy out cold with a knee to the side of the face.

Why am I telling you this? Bear with me one minute.

In New York City, an apparently wealthy New Jersey family sued the famed Plaza Hotel because the hotel cancelled a bas mitzvah for the family's daughter.

The Plaza was undergoing a massive renovation and the place had to be shuttered during a time when the party was scheduled to take place. So a few days after making the booking, the hotel called the family and broke the bad news.

The Plaza subsequently refunded the family's $12,000 deposit on the estimated $21,000 party (a Grrr! in and of itself), and also covered $2,060 for the family's costs for invitations, pins, and a family photo montage.

But that wasn't good enough, so they called a lawyer.

You see, the parents were both engaged and married at the Plaza, and the wife's brothers and sisters all celebrated their coming-of-age parties at the Plaza, as well.

It was a family tradition that they were understandably looking forward to sharing with their daughter. Most people can reasonably understand their disappointment.

But a lawsuit seeking unspecified damages for "humiliation, indignity, distress of mind, and mental suffering"?

The place was undergoing renovations, for crying out loud. These things happen. Start a new family tradition. Take up the Four Seasons. How about the Ritz? Surely there are other lavish places in which to begin new traditions.

But what does any of this have to do with Sammy Morgan getting knocked out? It goes right to the heart of what's wrong in our great nation—a nation of coddled citizens who throw tantrums in the form of lawsuits every time something doesn't go their way.

Morgan was competing for a six-figure contract to become a professional fighter in the UFC league. He was looking to make his dream come true, and with that came sacrifice. It meant leaving his jobs to train. It meant going to bed early, exercising like a madman, lifting weights, eating well—in other words, working hard for a better life, something fewer and fewer of us are doing to live the American Dream.

These days, we simply expect that dream to come true. We act like being born in this great country means we deserve all the things it stands for without the sacrifices they require.

When Sammy got his wits back after being knocked out, the realization that he was out of the competition and back to the drawing board hit him harder than Luke's knee.

"I didn't make it," he said. "I didn't make it."

Then the muscular fighter with the heart of gold and steel at once, a quiet man with an eye of a tiger, a man you'd want by your side in any dark alley anywhere in the world, cried his eyes out. He buried his face in his gloves and cried.

He then sought out his opponent and congratulated him on the win, and stood with his head high in the center of the ring while the ref announced Cummo the winner.

Sammy had class.

All the way across the country, in what is a world away from Sammy's reality, a wealthy and successful family is suing a storied establishment because their daughter won't be able to have her lavish party there. What kind of lesson do you think those parents are teaching their daughter?

I feel sorry for her. I'll take Sammy's way any day of the week. Nobody deserves anything, and when things don't work out, lick your wounds and find another way.

THE TRUMP CARD

Where's my trump card?

I mean, I wish that every time that I didn't get my way, I could blame someone. I wish that every time disaster strikes poor, little ol' me, I could point my finger to a specific reason why I'm so persecuted.

C. Virginia Fields, a New York Democratic mayoral candidate, blamed a lack of media coverage for her demise.

"I think the whole thing of not getting the kind of coverage by media on a lot of the issues that I know mattered to people and not getting that out in a way that I thought was important to me, that disappointed me," said Fields, the Manhattan borough president who was thinking about running for mayor of New York City.

Typical Grrring politician-speak, if you ask me.

Then there was Ty Taylor, the talented African-American singer who was booted off *Rock Star: INXS*. He blamed racism for his being voted off the show, which I can understand, because there are *no* minorities represented in the music industry. None at all.

Never mind the fact that two of the five winners of *American Idol* are African-American.

Ty, you're a great singer. You're just not a rock star. Go sing in *Rent.*

Remember Jayson Blair, the serial liar who sullied the reputation of *The New York Times* by fabricating quotes and whole stories?

Well, in his book—which I won't even name here for fear you might be tempted to waste your money on it—he blamed everything from depression to racism to drug and alcohol abuse.

It was never *his* fault.

Pete Rose blames the Javert-like pursuit of the late baseball commissioner Bart Giamatti for his lifelong ban from baseball, never once admitting he was gambling until he could profit from that admission in the form of a book deal.

But for nearly fifteen years it was Giamatti's fault.

Rafael Palmeiro, said that he never knew that the supplements that were supplied to him from various trainers or nutritionists were actually illegal, performance-enhancing substances.

Never mind the fact that he was taking Winstrol, which experts say cannot be confused with anything but steroids.

The whole concept of pointing fingers makes me want to break into song. Remember the Scarecrow's song in *The Wizard of Oz*, "If I Only Had A Brain"? Sing it like this:

> *If I only had a blame*
> *I could fail every minute,*
> *I would point at you infinitum,*
> *If I only had a blame.*

WHAT'S WRONG WITH GENERATION Z?

You want to know what's wrong with generations Y and Z? They're enabled by so many external forces, like pop culture and overprotective parents.

I came to this conclusion while dining at a chain restaurant staffed by college kids who looked like they were doing their parents a favor, rather than being there because they needed a job.

As I was thinking about how bad the service was, I heard a song by a group called Simple Plan titled "Welcome to My Life." It was all about being a loner, being misunderstood, picked on, and kicked when you're down.

Oh boo-hoo-hoo. Cry me a river.

This is what passes for popular music today, whiny little "woe is me"–type songs that enable all the little crybabies whose sense of entitlement just kills me. Look at me, I'm a cute intern wearing flip-flops and a tank top at the corporate office. Shouldn't you hire me because everyone thinks I'm cute?

Or, look at me, I'm a young punk whose mommy and daddy would only pay for the walk-up apartment when all of my friends live in doorman buildings. Shouldn't you hire me?

Now, obviously not every young person in this country is a little mama's boy or daddy's girl. Many are hard workers who know that it takes blood, sweat, and tears to get anywhere in this life. And guess what? No one will be there to save you when you're down.

Guess what? You will be kicked when you're down. You will feel lost. You will be on the edge of breaking down. Welcome to life, period.

Now grow up and get over it.

$$(((\quad 16 \quad)))$$

An Oblivion for All Seasons

OBLIVIONS OF SUMMER

Oblivions make me dread the beaches, pools, waterslides, and neighborhood barbeques during the hot summer months. Here's why:

◘ They'll kick sand on your just-oiled body as they haul the hoagie-filled cooler to their plot on the beach.

◘ You'll be hit unawares in the head with their football just as you're about to finish John Galt's manifesto in *Atlas Shrugged*, and you'll just nod and throw the ball back to them.

◘ They wear bathing suits they shouldn't be wearing, like bikinis or Speedos—enough on that point.

◘ They'll take a bite out of an undercooked burger, then throw it back on the grill.

◘ They'll pee in the pool.

◘ In that great big ocean they'll swim right next to you, or on that vast stretch of sand will set up camp right next to you.

◘ They'll run out on the baseball field and then cry foul when they get arrested and face jail time.

And let's not forget the Fourth of July. You ever notice the people who set off illegal fireworks are people you try to avoid making eye contact with while you're mowing your lawn? It's always the idiot in the crowd with the fireworks. I'm not talking about the professional pyrotechnicians involved with the big show. I'm talking about you. Yeah, you, the guy who is about to send off an e-mail to me about how you're safe with fireworks and that you have every right to set them off because you're patriotic.

You, who exercised his right until 3 A.M. because you thought nobody should be asleep on July 4. You, who impressed the preteens with your masculine demonstration of pyro-expertise by standing a beer bottle—which you just emptied into your oversized gut—on the street and inserting a bottle rocket into it. You're the same person who rides an ATV without a helmet late into the night and uses a loud leaf blower where a broom is sufficient. You're the same guy who flies Old Glory from his car antennae and seriously believes he won't be pulled over for speeding because he's a proud American.

You are an idiot. And please, before you fire off your e-mail, go outside and pick up your fireworks debris from the middle of your block.

Fireworks *are* a great way to celebrate Independence Day, but please remember to think of the safety of your spectators. Every year somebody inevitably gets hurt because some Obliviot thinks purchasing pyrotechnics is all that is required for shooting off a grand spectacle.

Fireworks are mini-explosives and are dangerous. I know this is obvious to most people, but all it takes is a little preparation and attention to detail to ensure everyone has a great time and no one gets hurt.

So please, consult a pyrotechnics professional or read up on fireworks safety at the National Council on Fireworks Safety Web site before lighting one single wick, www.fireworksafety.com.

I'm guilty of having too many power lawn tools. I have a John Deere that's a combination weed whacker with Aero-Flex head, hedge trimmer, and leaf blower. I also own a Craftsman ride-on lawn tractor and a Honda lawn mower.

Needless to say, my weekend warrior antics are loud. But listen, folks, I don't start working on my lawn before 8:00 A.M. Now, I know this is difficult in say, Arizona or Texas, but even Texans don't start with the power tools before 6:00 A.M., right?

Some people out there just start their engines way too early. There's nothing more Grrring then the neighborhood Oblivion who's blowing leaves and mowing grass at the crack of dawn.

I know you've got a 9:00 A.M. tee time, but give me a Grrring break, dude!

As if lawn care and fireworks aren't enough, I've got a friend whose neighbor installed speakers under the eaves in the back of his house, so he and his family can enjoy their native music from Armenia—loudly, I might add.

I keep telling my bud to call the cops, but he doesn't want to upset the neighborly "kwan" (as Rod Tidwell from *Jerry Maguire* would say). If you ask me, the kwan has already been upset, so he might as well go for it.

Why is it okay for our neighbors to get away with unneighborly behavior, but if we make a move to correct it, we feel bad? The Oblivions have us by the you-know-whats, that's why.

For those of you unlucky enough to live anywhere near a beach, you've probably noticed your supermarket is in shambles.

All the good cold cuts and meat are gone. There are shopping carts strewn all over the parking lots. There's no more milk or eggs, for crying out loud, and forget about the lines. They're epic.

Whenever people are "on vacation," they seem to turn into bigger Oblivions than they are when they're home. When did the word *vacation* become synonymous with *rude*?

I went to a fancy Jersey Shore restaurant on Memorial Day with the family and the in-laws, and it was like a combat zone. It was sheer bedlam. First of all, the kitchen was in the weeds, and our poor waitress was on the verge of tears.

But the noise level was at an all-time high.

No, I'm not a prude, and I'm not the guy screaming "get off my lawn," either. But there is a time and place for everything. Just because you and your little monsters have a long weekend doesn't mean you can behave like a moron.

OBLIVIONS OF WINTER

The first real blizzard of the winter might as well be Armageddon. At least that's what it looks like at the local supermarket and Home Depot.

Judging by the rash of shopping sprees right before the first snow of the season, it appears nobody owns a shovel, or rock salt (which is somewhat understandable), or an ice scraper for their cars.

Snowblowers blow out of Home Depot faster than the store could say, "twenty-five percent off." And the grocery store is a hundred times worse. What is it about snow that compels people to stock up on gallons and gallons of bottled water and milk, and dozens of eggs? Do they think the grocery store is going to be closed for a month after the snow is cleared? Is this the first time they've ever seen snow in their area?

Do they not know what to expect?

Look, folks, unless you live in an extremely rural area where the concept of a snowplow has yet to reach you . . . you need only stock up for one day, max. Come on, people! Suburbia is not going to end as you know it after a foot of snow. At the very least, don't wait 'til the last minute!

4 × 4 GRRRS

Here's just a friendly reminder to all the four-wheel-drive SUV owners blazing through the snow: your big tires and awesome hazardous-condition handling will not prevent your vehicle from skidding in the snow or ice after you hit the brakes.

Sure, your wheels don't spin in the snow. Sure, you can blow by any rear-wheel-drive sports car. Sure, you can get out of your driveway without shoveling. But you still have to stop after you get to where you're going, or at those pesky red lights, where a lot of you (and I'm included in the 4 × 4 crowd) skid into the rear ends of those stopped in front of you.

Please be more considerate of your fellow "snow mobilers" and slow down.

WEATHER REPORTS

So, it seems that when snow blankets a television station's market, the news directors send out their reporters to blanket the area with weather-related news coverage. That's all well and good, but wouldn't it be nice if the reporters actually talked to one another before filing their reports?

Every time it snows we see several back-to-back reports from different towns . . . and they are all exactly the same . . . just different names and different people. Each reporter stands in the driving snow, cowering under his or her hood. Each reporter asks a motorist: "How is it getting around in the snow?" Each reporter asks the sanitation worker in the plow truck: "How much snow have you plowed?" Each reporter goes to a supermarket and asks: "What did you stock up with?"

Same questions. Same answers. Different people. Thank goodness for football.

Bathroom Etiquette

o Cell phones should not be used in public bathrooms. There's nothing more disconcerting than being in the john and hearing someone having a phone conversation while sitting on the throne.

o Gents, when confronted with three empty urinals, please don't pick the one in the middle and force a coworker to have to squeeze in next to you to take a leak. Just pick the far one to relieve yourself.

o The "washing hands" rule does not only apply to restaurant workers. Seriously, how hard is it to wash your hands after doing your business?

o Ladies, don't talk to the person in the next stall. Let her pee in peace.

o Gents, once again, how difficult is it to clean the urine off the seat? It's seriously disgusting to enter a stall that has dried pee on the toilet.

o Please flush the toilet, and don't use so much toilet paper that you'll clog it up for the next guy.

o When there's a long line, like at a sports stadium, don't go in the out door and try to cut the line. One of these times someone is going to beat the living daylights out of you. I'm just warning you.

o Signs on restaurant bathroom doors should read simply MEN or WOMEN. Why? See those kids standing outside the bathroom scratching their heads, wondering if they're a BUCK or a FILLY? Nuff said.

Grrr!

Paris Hilton Is Trying to Ruin My Daughter, and More Reasons Why Hollywood Is Destroying Our Nation

What can you say about a girl who likes to perform sex acts on tape, who likes to date the sons of Greek millionaires, and has a trust fund worth a reported $50 million herself? What can you say about a girl who wears "Vote or Die" T-shirts and then doesn't vote but lives to tell about it?

What can you say about a girl named after a city and a hotel, who has absolute-zero talent and whose Q rating is minus 75 (which means she has no likability whatsoever)?

What can you say?

Can you say Paris Hilton is ruining our nation's youth? She is famous for being a no-talent hack who makes bad pornography movies in her spare time. She shows up everywhere there's a camera and thrives on cultivating the worst of what American pop culture has become: cheap and dirty.

The thing about Hilton that strikes me as odd is that she's not even the pretty sister. Nicky is so much better looking than Paris is, yet Paris gets all the attention. Oh, that's right, Nicky has class, which is a no-no among today's *It* girls. Between the years 2004 and 2005 it seemed the only thing anybody in the entertainment media could talk about was Paris Hilton. Who is she dating? What is she wearing? Is her diamond engagement ring real or a fake? What hamburger chain is she pitching? Why is she fighting with her *The Simple Life* costar Nicole Ritchie?

Around the same time Paris Hilton lost her Sidekick II phone, the telephone numbers of other rich and famous (some infamous) people were exposed for the world to see on the Internet. *The Insider* host Pat O'Brien had to change his number—not soon enough, I might add—after the respected host was caught in his own Paris Hilton–style controversy: He left drunken messages on his girlfriend's voice mail about how he would like to take advantage of her with a little help from his friends and cocaine.

Other numbers exposed included tennis star Anna Kournikova and Lindsay Lohan. In other words, Paris runs with a bunch of pretenders herself. Either that, or the tennis not-so-great and the Long Island temptress want to stay on good terms with Hilton in case they need her lawyer to broker a good deal for any one of their future sex tapes that happen to be "stolen" and subsequently acquired by an Internet distribution company.

Paris's sex tape with an ex-boyfriend not worth mentioning was downloaded millions of times. In fact, after the lawyers helped broker license fees for the amateur pornography—and it *was* amateur, from the lighting to the framing to the actual performing—it has become one of the highest grossing pornographic movies of all time.

But you can't call it a film.

You see, before Brad Pitt left Jennifer Aniston for Angelina Jolie, and after Ben Affleck left Jennifer Lopez for Jennifer Garner, there was nothing scandalous going on. The media were bored, and when the media are bored, they'll make stars out of whoever makes themselves available.

Paris was there when all the others weren't. Paris was there when we became tired of seeing the sunken eyes and the "I'm sorry" stare of repeated drug offender Robert Downey Jr. Paris was there while Michael Jackson was hiding away in Neverland, preparing for his child molestation trial. Paris was there when Gary Busey found God and stopped beating himself up, and Nick Nolte was sober.

Paris was there when Sean Penn stopped beating up photographers.
Paris was there when Jenna Jameson, the porn star, became as famous as any other celebrity. So if a porn star can make millions of dollars, write a best-selling book, and be featured on any television show talking about her porn career with pride and no regrets, what's left to be scandalous?

Well, an heiress who is also an heirhead, a media whore, and a bad porn star will fit the bill perfectly.

How ironic that when Hilton's star began to fade, she announced to a London tabloid that she was "not having sex for a year." In fact, she went on to state that she's decided kissing was okay, but she won't go any further because "I like the way guys go crazy when they can't have sex with you."

Wow. This is a woman who appears on MTV, *Access Hollywood*, *Entertainment Tonight*, and the E! Channel regularly. This is a woman who graces entertainment glossies and is quoted in tabloid papers and gossip columns.

In other words, this is a woman whom your impressionable-aged sons and daughters are overexposed to, and that's the kind of crap they're hearing. Now teenaged boys and ignorant men will think that it's okay for them to "go crazy" when a girl won't let them have sex with them, and girls are taught that it's fun to be teases.

Greatttttt.

NOTHING LEFT TO THE IMAGINATION

There was a time when being sexy meant leaving the steamy details to the audience's imagination. I don't mean to sound like a prude because I'm far from it, but when did having class go the way of the black and white TV set?

Thanks to all of the pop tarts and little come-hither actresses who are plastered everywhere, young girls are dressing as scantily as is allowed by law. And you can't even Grrr! the parents of these kids.

I've seen girls changing from the clothes their parents saw them leave home with, into their slut clothes in their friend's car in mall parking lots.

What is a parent to do, follow their kids to the mall? I guess so.

I'm not saying it's all Paris Hilton's fault. Surely Lindsay Lohan, Tara Reid, Britney Spears, and Jessica Simpson can take some of the blame. After the *Dukes of Hazzard* movie, you were hard-pressed to find a picture of Simpson where she wasn't wearing those tight-ass "Daisy Dukes" and a skimpy bikini top.

And little lip-synching sister Ashlee isn't much better when it comes to setting examples for her "millions" of fans.

I mean, was anyone surprised that Ashlee Simpson couldn't sing?

But we reap what we sow, don't we? I'm talking about the fifteen-minute culture of celebrity we live in today. The result is Simpson and any number of other manufactured pop stars, Real-ities, and two-dollar actors.

In case you were living under a rock in October 2004, "singer" Ashlee Simpson was caught with her microphone down—on her hip, actually—live on NBC's *Saturday Night Live* when the wrong backup vocal track played for her second performance of the night.

Simpson had planned to sing "Autobiography," but instead the lead vocals for "Pieces of Me," the song she "sang" earlier, played. Not knowing how to handle the technical snafu, Simpson danced a jig and took leave of the stage, leaving her band to play out the remainder of the segment.

SNL then cut to a commercial.

At the curtain call, Simpson inexplicably blamed her band for playing the wrong song. I guess that was just in case none of us had TiVo or weren't sober when the segment really played out. Hello!?

I'm sure her band was surprised to hear it was their fault that their lead singer is a phony, but then again she disses her own sister, Jessica, in a lot of her music, so the band shouldn't be surprised that when the Simpson hit the fan, Ashlee blamed somebody else. How very celebrity of her! And how ironic that the song that was supposed to play is titled "Autobiography."

A little telling, don't you think?

There used to be a time when one needed to prove oneself *before* getting a gig as big as *Saturday Night Live*. These days all you need is an established older sister (see Nicky or Jamie Lynn), a stylist, a record producer, and a song track to become a star.

ADULT CONTEMPORARY ACTORS

Adult Contemporary is a term used in commercial radio to describe light rock and roll and sappy love songs. It's a formula for the thirty-five-and-over demographic, although these days it's more like fifty and over.

But have you noticed that certain actors fall into the Adult Contemporary category after they reach a certain age and a certain purgatory in their careers? They're not quite dead, but they're not at all hot either. They're Adult Contemporary, like the soft rock radio stations that use the word *Lite* in their call signs.

James Caan is Adult Contemporary. So are Rob Lowe, Melanie Griffith, Mimi Rogers, Valerie Bertinelli, Sharon Stone, and David Caruso. Even Caruso's character on *CSI: Miami* is AC. Just look at the bio from the show's official Web site:

[Horatio] Caine entered the police academy after high school, but quickly discovered that the beat left him bored. When he realized that the evidence-cracking CSIs were the people who actually solved the crimes, he enrolled in [a] university and, four years later, Chemistry degree in hand, he was a Level I Criminalist with the Miami-Dade Police Department.

See what I mean? And did the great Jerry Bruckheimer approve that copy?

Hey Caruso, here's a news flash for you:

Russell Crowe stole your act. He stole it right out of *Night and the City* and *King of New York*. He took your tough guy persona, put it in *L.A. Confidential,* and you haven't been hired to carry a movie since. Of course, you didn't help your cause when you walked off *NYPD Blue.* Russell Crowe should be paying royalties to you, instead of buying his way out of assault charges—by way of phone in New York City. But Russell Crowe will never be Adult Contemporary. Not after *Gladiator,* a.k.a., "David Caruso in a skirt."

Adult Contemporary actors can't sell movie tickets, but they do well on Broadway.

You see, there are enough suckers who will pay top dollar to see any star while they're in New York City for the holidays to keep the union stagehands employed for at least six more months. And after the end of Rosie O'Donnell's run in *Fiddler On The Roof,* some other Broadway producer with a Britney Spears or a Mary Tyler Moore project in tow comes into town with a fistful of dollars.

It's only a matter of time before Paris Hilton, the sizzling hot, red-carpet publicity whore who can afford nice clothes but actually gets paid to wear them, who can afford a bottle of Cristal but actually gets paid to drink it, who can afford a pair of Jimmy Choos but gets paid to hide her talons in them, will become Adult Contemporary, and after her Broadway debut she'll get a sitcom with Tony Danza.

Tony Danza is not only Adult Contemporary, he's cheesy.

I saw him do a one-man act (it was so bad I can't bring myself to call it a show) at Feinstein's in New York City. In the act, Danza—

whose audience that night included showbiz icon Liza Minnelli (gasp!)—performs a stand-up routine, talks about his days as a boxer, plays the trumpet, sings Sinatra songs, tap-dances, and speaks Italian.

What a Renaissance man! I could hardly contain my awe.

I kept waiting for one of Tony's old Brooklyn Italian aunts to stand up at the back of the lounge and scream, "Show them the backflip, Tony!"

Danza needs a John Travolta *Pulp Fiction* type comeback if he wants to get off the C-list of celebrities, but I don't think even Quentin Tarantino can bring Danza back from Adult Contemporary purgatory. Danza should have studied Ted Danson's career, instead of Regis Philbin's. At least he'd still have some dignity.

Regis Philbin is hands-down the coolest guy on television.

He can sing well enough. He's funny. He interviews celebrities better than anyone in the business, including Letterman and Leno, and he's a perfect foil for the lovely Kelly Ripa.

Tony Danza wants to be Regis Philbin, but he should go home and get his shine box.

The thing that makes Philbin so good is that he looks like he's enjoying the ride. He looks like the type of guy who if his career ended tomorrow would say, "What took them so long?" That's the guy we want in our living rooms day in and day out. Not Danza, who probably calls his agent daily to ask "Why don't they like me? I'm funny. I can sing. I can act. I can play the trumpet. Listen, I'll show you." All the while, when Danza's tooting his horn, the agent is on another line booking Ryan Seacrest for another hosting gig. Danza, out.

Eric Bogosian of *SubUrbia* fame is no better.

In Winter of 2006, I caught his act, *This Is Now*, where he was joined by jazz artist Elliott Sharp, who is widely regarded as one of New York's downtown music sensations. Sharp combines rock, blues, and classical music with a jazz improvisation that alone will hold your attention, but added to Bogosian's pop-culture rants should give you a show that will blow your socks off.

Unfortunately, for me, while Bogosian has always been one of my favorites when it comes to humor and sharp wit, I think listening to William Hung's greatest-hits collection might have been more entertaining.

If I wanted a lecture on how bad we greedy, self-centered, warmongering Americans are, I could have picked up a copy of *The New York Times* and called it a day.

Firstly, *This Is Now* was old, regardless of the immediacy Bogosian's title invokes. I kept waiting for an original thought to come off the stage, and aside from one really cool riff by Sharp on guitar—which incidentally reminded me of the scene in *Kung Fu Hustle* when the old Chinese sitar player throws invisible daggers at opponents during his tune—Bogosian's rants might have been culled from conspiracy Web sites after 9/11.

Not only that, but when referring to stereotypical black movie characters he used quotes from Ving Rhames's *Pulp Fiction* character to illustrate his point of how America forces Hollywood to stereotype because it only accepts blacks in certain roles.

"I'm going to get medieval on your ass," Bogosian quotes. Okay, point taken, but I saw this show in 2006. Ten years after *Pulp Fiction* came out. Surely he could have found more recent examples of stereotyping, no?

Secondly, I couldn't help but notice how old Bogosian looked, and from my seat, looking at a graying man going off on stage like some naïve college kid is not as charming as watching some naïve college kid going off on stage.

The performance left me wondering why Bogosian would subject himself to the exercise. Does he think his fans need a good lecturing— or did he simply feel the need to preach to the choir?

After this show, I needed a stiff drink, so I stopped at Nick and Tony's, an Italian restaurant just up the block from the Merkin Theater in New

York City, where *This Is Now* was playing. Since Oblivion encounters often happen in threes for me, whom do I sit next to at the bar?

None other than Tony Danza, having dinner and drinks with a soap star pal. This in and of itself is nothing to Grrr about, until he got up to leave and his pal announced to the restaurant and its staff, "Tony Danza is leaving, ladies and gentlemen."

"Yes, Tony Danza is leaving," Danza said, as he took a bow, blew a kiss, and stumbled out the front door.

I couldn't help but laugh to myself, and I had to refrain from yelling out, "Show them the backflip, Tony!"

SMILE, YOU'RE ON PAPARAZZI CAMERA . . .

A Grrr! reader wrote me an e-mail in the summer of 2006 about how actress Lindsay Lohan is always crying about getting her picture taken by paparazzi, but if she really wanted to avoid them, she wouldn't be eating lunch at The Ivy every day, where photographers and stargazers linger for celebrity photos.

Coincidentally I was in Santa Monica one week after reading that e-mail, walking down Ocean Boulevard, right past The Ivy, and guess who was sitting in the window, laughing and throwing her hair back, grabbing my attention as I walked by the patio windows. Yup, Lindsay Lohan, front and center.

Now, celebrities are entitled to their privacy, and I won't deny that the paparazzi do go overboard from time to time. But not all photographers are bad people, and if they were, then all celebrities would avoid red carpets. They don't. And that's because most celebs need to see their pictures on the covers of magazines and their names on Page Six often. They need it because some public relations person is telling them it's good for their career, then taking a few grand every month for the advice.

Still, other celebrities make their living taking pictures, particularly supermodels, like the ones in the Victoria's Secret lingerie catalogue and who bless the pages of *Sports Illustrated*'s Swimsuit Edition.

These women are ultrasexy, there's no denying that.

But what is with the attitude on these supermodels? They get paid a shitload of money to wear clothes and walk on a runway. They don't walk so much as strut. It's like an art form; however, give me a Balanchine ballet any day of the week.

Isn't it funny how a ballet dancer is relegated to a short career at Lincoln Center where the only people who will ever notice her are ballet aficionados and subscribers. Meanwhile, supermodels are world-famous but have very little to offer other than soft-porn photos for young boys to gawk at and young girls to try to emulate.

And not in a good way, either.

Ask any supermodel if they actually like what they do and you won't get an honest answer. They like the money, yes. Some may even revel in the fame. But constant dieting, smoking, or worse, just ask Kate Moss, to keep the hunger pangs at bay, and wearing designer duds that barely cover their butts gets old real fast.

Meanwhile girls are making themselves throw up after meals because they think they have to look like the girl on the magazine cover.

FASHION WEEK

I've covered a few fashion shows during New York City's Fashion Week, and I'll tell you, I have never seen three-quarters of the clothes that make it down the runway on any person's back in real life.

I know, I know. I just don't understand fashion. You're right. Give me a classic pair of Sears jeans and a classic, solid, three-button Joseph Abboud or Calvin Klein suit any day of the week. They will still be in style long after the leather hot pants for men and the J.Lo number for women disappear from MTV.

Just who designers are making clothes for these days is beyond me. And whoever pays more than forty bucks for a pair of jeans is an idiot. I'm sorry, but I can't tell the difference between a pair of Levi's from Marshall's and a pair of $200 Lucky Brand jeans from the Lucky shop at The Groves shopping center in Los Angeles.

Every time I go to Los Angeles and end up working with women I seem to get the same compliment time and again.

"It's so nice to meet a man, as opposed to the man-boys we work with and meet day in and day out here."

It's a sad testament to our times when a man being a man is so rare it bears complimenting on. Wow.

And to think I'm wearing classic suits or $15 Canyon River Blues jeans from Sears! Although, how much of my "manliness" actually has anything to do with my clothes? I tell them I just happen to be comfortable in my own skin, like so many other "manly" men.

All of the Hollywood wannabes might have actually made it already if they were brave enough to be comfortable in their own skins.

Trying to be like everybody else is what's holding them back.

I'll tell you, I don't miss acting. I don't miss sitting in a some audition waiting area hearing the same stories from the same wannabes every day.

"Quentin's got my script."

"I'm reading for David Chase for that thing."

"What agent are you with?"

I've left several auditions before even auditioning because I was embarrassed that the career I was choosing put me in the same category with some of the dumbest, most egocentric people on the planet. A lot of actors are so self-centered they make even the most egregious Oblivions seem tame in comparison.

Ask any non-"in-the-business" woman who has ever dated an actor if the guy ever actually saw her. Chances are he was too busy looking at his reflection in whatever surface afforded him the view, or he was looking over her shoulder to see if there was anybody in the room he could use to help further his career.

Actresses are even worse, because they know they can bat their eyelashes at a producer and can flirt their way into a movie. Some even go further.

Hollywood can be great for people who have their heads screwed on tight. But the majority of people coming to this town believe that once they arrive at LAX some talent scout for CAA is just waiting for them in the airport lobby. These are the folks who give acting a bad name. And sadly, there's hundreds arriving every day.

"Look at me." "Look at me." Heaven forbid one of them steps in shit and actually makes it. They know who you should vote for and what kind of car you should drive before you know. But they don't even realize that people are pulling their little puppet strings from on high. No idea.

Oblivions.

Watch Out for Orexiaorexia

Look out, Scandalgate.

The new disease about to sweep the nation is Orexia-orexia.

The birth of the term *tanorexia,* which describes people who can't get enough skin coloring and spend way too much time either at tanning booths, in the sun, or rubbing orange-tinged creams all over their bodies, had journalists everywhere frothing at their keyboards.

But tanorexia and its skin-damaging effects are the least of our problems.

Our biggest Grrrs will come when some unoriginal news copywriter starts putting an *-orexia* or *-orexic* at the end of every addictive condition, much like the suffix *-gate* is added to every scandal.

No longer will Watergate, Memogate, Monicagate, or Paulagate dominate the teleprompter.

We news consumers will now be subjected to words like *colarexic* for kids who drink too much cola. *Shoporexic* will replace the equally unoriginal *shopaholic* and *pokerexia* will describe those who can't stop playing Texas Hold'em.

Texto-rexia describes the constant text messaging that occurs on cell phones, two-way pagers and Blackberries.

DIYO-rexics are people who are addicted to *Extreme Makeover* and other home improvement shows.

Video-rexia will refer to PlayStation 2 and Xbox addicts, as well as MTV junkies.

Grrr!

Continued

Travelexia describes people who take more than two vacations every year.

Weborexics are people who are constantly online.

Grrr-orexics are people who are addicted to the "Grrr!" column; previously known as *Grrr-pies.*

The weird part about using *tanorexia* and *tanorexic* to describe people who tan too much is that anorexics are people who don't eat enough. Wouldn't it be better to describe chronic tanners as *tanoholic*?

Oh well, orexic and *orexia* will become so customary that eventually *anorexia* will lose its cachet and go the way of alcoholism. It will become *anorexism*.

THEY ALL LOOK ALIKE

I saw a great picture of Nicole Kidman in the *New York Post* one weekend. I was thinking, darn, she looks better and better every year. And then I read the caption.

The photo was of Jude Law's embattled honey, Sienna Miller.

Sienna Miller?

She looked just like Nicole Kidman in the shot. In fact, that happens a lot. I interviewed Cindy Crawford at an Ultimate Fighting event and someone asked me what it was like to interview Julia Roberts. I said I never did. The person insisted that I interviewed the *Pretty Woman* star. I was flabbergasted. Could I have forgotten an interview with Roberts? I highly doubt it, but stranger things have happened.

After further investigation, it was the Crawford interview the person was talking about. "They all look alike," he said. I agree.

If you think about it, a lot of famous women look alike. Reese Witherspoon (my girlfriend, as my wife calls her) looks like Kelly Clarkson. Emmy Rossum of *Phantom of the Opera* fame is interchangeable with *The Princess Diaries* star Anne Hathaway. Paris Hilton looks like Ruth Buzzi. Mischa Barton (*The O.C.*) looks like Tom Cruise's paramour, Katie Holmes. Jenna Jameson, the porn star, looks like Pamela Anderson. Rachel McAdams (*The Notebook*) can star in any Kate Bosworth (*Win A Date With Tad Hamilton*) movie. Kelly Ripa (also my girlfriend, according to my wife), looks like Charlize Theron—well, not really, but Charlize *is* my girlfriend.

Okay, I'm digressing big time, but you get the point.

Back to Sienna Miller for a minute. A lot of people might be wondering why she did not leave Jude Law after he had sex with the nanny. My theory is as jaded as Grrr!, so take it with a grain of salt.

While Miller is somewhat famous in England, did you ever hear of her before the Jude Law/nanny sexcapades? Nope. My theory is that the whole darn sex-with-the-nanny thing was a total setup to boost Miller's career. Think about it. Everywhere you turn you see Sienna Miller these days.

Law not only used the nanny for a roll in the hay, he also used her to manipulate the media into making his fiancée a star. They must have taken a page out of the Hugh Grant/Elizabeth Hurley scandal book.

While Hurley was already semifamous as a model, did you ever hear so much about her before Grant was arrested for getting a hummer from a prostitute in La La Land? Nope. That little transgression made Hurley's career even bigger, because all rational human beings could not fathom how Grant could choose a prostitute named Divine to cheat on Hurley with.

Hollywood playbook, Chapter two.

Real-ities and Other
TV "Personalities"

What can you say about a bunch of Oblivions who are not only oblivious to their surroundings, but also live day in and day out in a sycophantic, insular environment that fosters and caters to their insecure egos?

Now imagine we're talking about Reality TV stars!

Just regular Joes like you and me who happen to have applied to the right contest that put them on a national stage. These are people so repugnant they don't see a problem with living in a house full of strangers in front of millions of viewers.

Real-ities make celebrities seem like the most secure, stable, and morally guided people in the world, and we all know that's nonsense.

But some people who have had their taste of fame, no matter how fleeting, find it very difficult to let go.

Omarosa, anyone? Surely you remember the Queen Bitch from the first season of Donald Trump's television show *The Apprentice*.

She's the one who played the race card as soon as things didn't go her way. After she heard those famous words "You're fired" from Mr. Trump and lost her weekly run on national television, she said a white woman on the show called her the N word and after making news headlines, hitting the tabloids, news channels, late night and daytime talk show circuits running, she began spreading rumors about how she was entertaining several offers from TV networks and production companies wanting her to do a talk show.

We're still waiting for that gabfest.

I'll give her this: Omarosa knew how to manipulate the media. Even the mighty Oprah Winfrey played right into her hands, allowing Omarosa to share the talk show queen's stage with Donald Trump, when others from the show, including Erika Vetrini, the woman wrongfully accused of using the N word, sat in the audience with a stick microphone.

What a joke. And Oprah went down a few notches in my book after that.

Anyway, Omarosa thankfully disappeared into the not-so-quiet night and resurfaced on a new show called *Battle of the Reality Stars*. There she served as sideline reporter during such events where, for instance, a midget from CBS's *Amazing Race* got pounded to a pulp by a woman from another reality show as they tried to displace one another off of a balance beam into a pool of water.

Omarosa was so uncomfortable on camera she was even more embarrassing to watch then the actual show was.

"Oma, Oprah. Oprah, Oma." (A little tribute to David Letterman's tragic Oscar hosting.)

But *The Apprentice* wasn't the first big reality hit.

It was of course, CBS's *Survivor*, which had its share of Obliviots. Remember Richard Hatch, a.k.a. the Naked Cowboy?

Hatch was so excited about being on television that he romped around the island in his birthday suit, hairy ass, and huge love handles exposed for the world to see. He eventually won the million-dollar prize.

But guess what? He never reported the income to the I.R.S. Here's a guy who won big-time money in front of more than forty million people, and he didn't report the prize.

Hatch said taxes were the obligation of CBS. Nope. He went to jail.

And then there's "Cabby," a Howard Stern crony from the popular radio program who also served time after going on the air and bragging about how he never pays taxes on considerable income. What an idiot!

The lesson here is, don't fool with the I.R.S., because you will lose, whether you are famous or not.

But Omarosa, Cabby, and Hatch are just three of many Real-ities we were so unfortunate to have in our living rooms. Another one was Rob Campos of NBC's short-lived *For Love or Money*.

In case you were one of the one billion people who didn't see the show, the premise of this train wreck was the show's star—Campos— chose a woman out of a dozen or so to date on a permanent basis. But there was a twist: the woman he chose could dump him if she'd rather have the money.

I think the take was a hundred grand.

Since the venerable *Today* morning show on NBC is nothing more than a corporate commercial for the network's prime-time lineup these days, it was not surprising that Katie Couric interviewed Rob Campos before the show's premiere episode.

In the interview, Campos had just commented that he would have picked Couric were she one of the women contestants on the show. *He's hitting on her!* I thought. How typically arrogant of this Obliviot Reality.

To her credit, Couric brushed him off and moved along without even cracking a smile. She saw right through him. And, through her eyes, so could everyone watching.

During the run of the show, we learned through some intrepid reporting that appeared on thesmokinggun.com that Campos—a former marine—was expelled from the Marine Corps Judge Advocate General (JAG) training program after he drunkenly groped the breasts of a female navy officer.

Hello Frisco!

The navy put him on administrative punishment and ordered him to enroll in a substance abuse treatment program.

Campos neglected to disclose this little fact to NBC—presumably because he knew he would get the boot yet again, this time from a national television show. He reportedly told a private investigator working for the program that there was "absolutely nothing" irregular about his JAG service.

Earlier in the Couric interview, Campos said his mom was skeptical and a little embarrassed about his fledgling reality TV career, but that she was slowly warming up to the idea.

He should have listened to her.

Mom knew better. Mom knew that little Robbie should leave well enough alone. She knew her handsome boy had fooled enough people to get by okay. Why rock the boat?

"I thought it was a private matter," Campos told The Smoking Gun Web site, referring to the groping incident. "I thought it was over."

Campos's bio was quickly removed from NBC's Web site. The Dallas law firm where he worked also had his bio, which mentioned his service in the JAG. Not only did the law firm remove Campos's bio, they fired him.

One thing we all know from reality show experience (Sarah Kozer's foot fetish video, anyone?), when one signs on to participate on a reality show, there are no private matters.

Even though we TV viewers are becoming less and less choosy as to whom we invite into our living rooms, we still want to know what kind of people they are up front.

But not all Real-ities are bad people.

The aforementioned Erika Vetrini ended up as a sidekick for Tony Danza for one season, but she was unceremoniously let go when the show tanked in the ratings. Surely that had *nothing* at all to do with the show's cheesy host!

Vetrini resurfaced as a business correspondent on CNBC, GRRRing, but she did study broadcast journalism.

Real-ities who get broadcasting jobs after getting some national exposure used to be a major Grrr! for me. But I have to admit, who among us wouldn't take a job on national television, qualified or not?

That's the thing about reality shows. Boston Rob from *Survivor* is making regular appearances on CBS's *The Early Show,* and if not for the exposure on these reality shows, these cohosting and contributor jobs might actually go to broadcasters who have paid their dues in the business. Instead, network executives are looking for the quick bang for their buck, and to hell with integrity.

Of course, the Real-ities who really take the cake are the pretenders who are so hell-bent on becoming famous that they do some irrational things to get on television. Why the hell anyone would ever agree to appear on *Fear Factor* is beyond me. Could you imagine eating pig stomach or letting eels envelop your body, all for a measly couple-thousand-dollars prize and the chance to be on national television?

But TV does have that power, doesn't it?

Just look at the Oblivions who hold up signs outside the windows of the morning show studios and at MTV's Times Square studios daily. The worst ones are the people who have no clue what the anchors are talking about, yet act like morons in the background, anyway.

I was watching one morning show after Hurricane Katrina, and as the anchors were talking about the devastation suffered in the Gulf States, some jackass in the background waved his hand profusely while keeping a cell phone glued to his ear.

"Do you see me? Do you see me?" Yeah dude, they see you. We all see you. You're an Obliviot.

Then there are the Real-ities who show up anywhere there's a camera. These folks make Tom Arnold look camera-shy. It's amazing. I find Tom Arnold wherever I happen to be on assignment with a camera. I covered the Consumer Electronics Show in Las Vegas and Tom Arnold was there, hawking some product and competing with Jackie Chan for some camera time. A month later I was covering parties at the Super Bowl and sure enough, there was Arnold. The following year at the Consumer Electronics Show—guess who? A month later at an Oscars preparty I was covering, yup, Tom Arnold. The guy knows where to be seen, that's for sure.

But at least Arnold is a celebrity and, seriously, a hoot to be around (at least when cameras are rolling—isn't every celebrity)?

I covered a press announcement for a new Broadway show called *Chef's Theater* one summer—where celebrity chefs appeared in a dinner theater setting. It was like experiencing a Food Network TV show taping with live music and singing performed by pasty white Broadway rejects. It was a terrible idea and I had to refrain from laughing out loud during the press conference as the pock-faced producer proclaimed that the next big thing in New York theater had arrived.

The show closed after two weeks.

Anyway, Kwame Jackson, the runner-up from the first season of *The Apprentice* was there, and his publicist came up to me and asked me if I wanted a sound bite from Jackson? I asked, "Is he in it?"— meaning the musical. "No, he's just here showing his support," was the publicist's answer. So I asked if Jackson knew the producer or anyone else associated with the next big thing in New York theater. He said no.

At a loss trying to figure out what a reality-show contestant was doing showing support for a show he had nothing to do with, I declined my opportunity for sound with Jackson. What the hell did Kwame Jackson have to do with this show? Nothing. Absolutely nothing. But his two-dollar publicist probably told him, "Dude, there's gonna be press, let's just go there."

Not on my watch, Dude. In fact, I treated the Hilton sisters exactly the same way before they were the toast of *Access Hollywood* and Page Six. Whenever I covered red carpet arrivals for movie premieres, celebrity charity events, or awards shows, some publicist would escort Nicky and Paris Hilton to my camera and microphone so that I could have the privilege of interviewing them. I'd always wave them by.

What was I supposed to ask them? What is it like to live off of Granddaddy's dime?

But I digress.

REALITY TV = MEAN

The truth hurts. Nice guys finish last.

I'm talking about Sir Richard Branson, the star of the short-lived FOX reality series, *The Rebel Billionaire.*

After two weeks on the air, the ratings for the Virgin mogul's foray into Donald Trump–land fell flatter than quirky *Apprentice 2* star Raj Bhakta's attempt to get Robin—Trump's trusty assistant—to go out on a date with him.

The problem with *The Rebel Billionaire* was that Branson was too nice—and in television, nice doesn't work.

Even though *The Apprentice* lost considerable ratings over the seasons, millions of people still tuned in each week to hear those two signature words from Mr. Trump: "You're fired."

By contrast, Richard Branson sent losing contestants home with a genuinely great smile and a hug. Nope. Not gonna work.

Whether one is in front of the TV cameras or somewhere in the control room, mean is what the audience wants. I don't mean "mean for the sake of being mean." There's a time and place for mean, and when that time and place is right, there's no better television.

Like when *The Daily Show*'s Jon Stewart skewered former CNN *Crossfire* cohosts Paul Begala and Tucker Carlson—on their own set—just before the 2004 election. The conversation turned into confrontation, and when things got real mean, they got real good.

Or when former New York Yankee Chad Curtis declined to speak with sports broadcaster Jim Gray "out of respect for Pete [Rose]" after Curtis hit a World Series walk-off home run. Gray had been lambasted for trying to get Rose to admit he gambled on baseball on a night when Rose was actually being honored.

Thousands cheered Curtis as a red-faced Gray tossed back to Bob Costas in the booth. Never mind the fact that Gray was right, but Rose only admitted as much when he had a book to sell.

Behind the scenes, stories of actors being disciplined by big-media meanies for not reporting to work during contract negotiations abound, from producer Dick Wolf's near firing of the stars of one of his series, *New York Undercover,* several years ago—to CBS's Les Moonves's not-so-subtle message to *CSI* stars Jorja Fox and George Eads after the two staged an apparent sick-out (it was all a big "misunderstanding," the actors said—sure).

The bottom line is, Simon Cowell is the king of Reality Television, for one reason only.

You guessed it. He's mean.

Here is a list of people who, after their careers crash and burn, can easily make the transition into Reality Television:

Kobe Bryant in . . . *I Thought What Happens on the Road Stays on the Road*

Martha Stewart in . . . *Cool Hand Martha*

Michael Jackson in . . . *Neverland Was Never This Hot*

Madonna in . . . *Horsey Don't Preach*

J.Lo/Ben Affleck in . . . *Good Will Hogging*

Dennis Kozlowski in . . . *The Party That Launched a Thousand Years*

Bernie Ebbers in . . . *MC Why Why Why?*

Britney Spears in . . . *When Pigs Fly*

Scott Peterson in . . . *How I Killed Your Mother*

Janet Jackson in . . . *Nipple Me This, Batman*

Jesse Palmer in . . . *The Bachelor Sacked My Football Career*

Jayson Blair in . . . *White Man Keeping Me Down*

"Scooter" Libby in . . . *This Is Your CIA*

Tom Cruise in . . . *Top Nut*

I'm sure I'm missing several, but the list changes with time. Remember the Tonya Harding/Nancy Kerrigan saga? By the time Kerrigan won her silver medal I was fantasizing about taking a pipe to her other knee if I had to see that "Why me" video one more time. "Why, why, why?"

But I digress.

Remember questions like: Is Kobe innocent or guilty? How much time should Martha serve? Will Madonna suck face with Britney again? Or, will she continue to write children's books? Personally, I can't believe the same person is doing both, but hey, she's loaded, so that makes it okay. Madonna, just go away. Stay in sunny London.

As for Jennifer Lopez: at least she and husband, Marc Anthony, have kept somewhat of a low profile, despite the fact that at a Grammy Award show they sang a duet in Spanish about how they wished people would just leave them alone.

Rich Does Not Make Right

We're all guilty of letting someone's fat wallet cloud our otherwise good judgment at one time or another. How many times have these words come out of your mouth: "Yeah, but he's loaded."

Seems like no matter how much of an Oblivion a perceived rich person may be, we little people are always willing to forgive her for whatever indiscretions.

That's why the Martha Stewart verdict was so shocking. I guess those twelve jurors were not under the misguided impression that Martha would have paid off every one of their mortgages had they acquitted her. Good for them for "keeping it real." (I hate that phrase but I needed to make the point as obnoxiously as possible.)

One of my favorite urban legends . . .

A guy (he's an electrician, plumber, Kinko's employee—whatever) is driving down the New Jersey Turnpike during a rainstorm, when he sees a limousine driver fixing a flat. The guy pulls over to help and, lo and behold, none other than Donald Trump exits the stretch with a hundred dollar bill for his troubles. Guy says, "Keep the money, but here's my card. Please send my wife flowers because she'll never believe this." A few weeks go by and still no flowers, but wait—a letter from the bank. The Donald paid off his mortgage.

Yeah, right. Grrr! to the pipe dreamers. But speaking of The Donald, even he is perplexed at the fact that he rarely has to pay for a meal. Here is a guy who can well afford to

Grrr!

Continued

pay for dinner at any restaurant in the world, but the owners of said places won't charge him. It's unbelievable.

Donald Trump said this in *Playboy* magazine on not having to pay for meals at fancy restaurants: "'Oh please, Mr. Trump. There's no charge.'–Even if I'm with ten or fifteen people. The sad part is, if I were someone who needed money I'd have to pay."

And therein lies the Grrr!

Restaurants and other like establishments are so desperate for celebrity business that the rich and famous never have to pay. It's so commonplace that even when millionaire celebs do get charged, they get offended: "Do you know who I am?"

As a matter of fact, yes we do. And that's why you'll pay. You can afford it.

As for Trump, at least he has the wherewithal to tip well when he's comped. I wish more Oblivion celebs remembered to tip their servers, including the Bush twins, who reportedly left a $48 tip on a $5,000 bar tab that was comped at a nightclub when the ladies were in New York City during the Republican National Convention. And I'm a big fan of all the Bush women, from First Lady Laura to Jenna and Lauren, but Grrr! on you two for that move.

Did I mention they sang that song about their lack of privacy on national television?

As for the CEO convicts, like Koslowski and Ken Lay (who died of a heart attack before he would have surely been sentenced to several years in prison), their cases were a victory for the little people.

I mean, how greedy can you get? The judges showed no mercy on these guys. There will be no more million dollar parties for Kozlowski, and to add insult to injury, in the summer of 2006, the wife he threw that Greek shindig for filed for divorce. Ouch.

The Koz should just go to jail at Baghdad's Abu Ghraib. They can send an eight thousand dollar dog leash so that he can be "tortured" at the hands of the U.S. Army in the style he was accustomed to.

I never thought I'd be saying this, but give me Jessica Simpson over Britney Spears any day of the week. Here I thought that one day Jessica would be on top of my Grrr! list, but then Britney goes and gets married and unmarried in one day, locks lips with Madonna, and is now remarried to a man who has two kids with another woman . . . and they say Christina Aguilera and Tara Reid have morals issues?

This just in: The other day I was perusing a celebrity event press release when I came across the name of fourteen-year-old soccer phenom Freddie Adu.

Get this. Young Freddie, who had played just a handful of professional soccer games at this time, was being honored as an "innovator," along with the likes of David Bowie. Now David Bowie I can see as an innovator. But Freddie Adu? Give the kid a chance.

The point is, it's kind of hard to Grrr! Real-ities and Celebrity Oblivions when everybody around them keeps putting them up to public scrutiny, all in the name of some big-money endorsement that all of these people collect a percentage of. It's no wonder Paris Hilton shows up at every party imaginable. She's being paid to, and her booker is cashing in, too.

NEW REALITY SHOW: *CON MAN WITH JAYSON BLAIR*

It's only a matter of time, so don't be surprised when you find Jayson Blair hosting his very own reality show.

He may not have Monica Lewinsky appeal (yes, that's a joke), but with a book deal chronicling his massive fraud as an up-and-coming reporter for *The New York Times,* Blair might find his fifteen minutes of fame stretched to fifteen episodes of gut-wrenching television.

I can see it already:

An unwitting pedestrian walking through Times Square "bumps" into Blair, in costume as a street punk. Blair drops a day-old hamburger on the sidewalk and begins screaming about how the man owes him ten dollars for the lunch that just fell out of his hands.

Not knowing he's being scammed, the pedestrian forks over the guilt money to make good for his apparent goof. Game, set, match: Blair.

"Stay tuned next week when our unscrupulous host tries his luck with an ATM scam," an announcer voices.

Since the story of his misdeeds broke on the front page of *The New York Times* a few years ago, Blair had been analyzed by psychology experts, had bragged about his premeditated plagiarisms and fabrications, and had shamelessly played the race card (the title for his book is *Burning Down My Master's House*). Never mind the fact that Howell Raines, the executive editor of *The New York Times,* was faulted for giving Blair *preferential treatment!*

A more appropriate title might be *Suspend Your Disbelief.*

What this unfortunate circumstance really boils down to, however, is pure and unadulterated laziness by someone who squandered the opportunity of a lifetime.

It is not easy to break into the world of elite media.

It calls for sweat equity that rivals Olympic competition. It requires long hours and sacrifice, low starting pay, and a desire and commitment to the product, to oneself, and to colleagues.

Rejection is as common in this business as being asked to make coffee runs. So resilience and persistence are prerequisites that aren't taught and can't be learned. There are no shortcuts.

Blair lied his way up the ladder, and after reading the writing he himself wrote on the wall, decided to light a match and bring it all down with him, lest he be justly fired without incident—and more to the point, without compensation.

In a world where a Florida woman hires an attorney because her cell phone number happens to be the same as one that appeared in the blockbuster movie *Bruce Almighty*, causing her to suffer—brace yourself—an excessive amount of phone calls—too many people these days are looking for too many shortcuts.

It's time the nonsense stops.

ROCK STAR: INXS

Which is why I loved CBS's 2005 summer replacement show *Rock Star: INXS*, where hosts Brooke Burke and Dave Novarro joined the iconic '80s band in their search for a new lead singer.

Like FOX's *American Idol*, this show featured performers who put their dreams on the line in front of millions of people, and for that I admire them. But both shows suffer from TMI—Too Much Information.

Perhaps the most disturbing part of the *American Idol* controversy involving Paula Abdul's alleged affair with contestant Corey Clark was the flood of sordid details.

Not only did Clark reveal to all who would listen the tale of his broken heart at the hands of his celebrity lover, he also put to rest the notion that "a gentleman never tells."

While FOX announced that the *American Idol* judge would be allowed to stay on with the show because it found no cause for dismissal, enough dirty laundry was aired to the point that many of us never want to hear another word about Abdul.

Which brings me back to *Rock Star: INXS*.

Despite poor ratings, *Rock Star* was a great show. If you like seeing people put themselves out there to make their dreams come true, then this is right up there with *American Idol,* and hosts Brooke Burke and Dave Navarro are a lot prettier than Ryan Seacrest, if that's even possible. I mean come on, Novarro is so freakishly pretty he must have been a woman in a past life.

Now, if you followed the show at all, you might have observed that J. D. Fortune had the rock star look, including the requisite tattoos and smoldering stare.

J. D. was also extremely good at arranging songs to fit his singing style, and he took risks with his performances. One could argue he was the most musically talented of them all.

But it was too late for J. D. Fortune long before the season finale. During the show, he came across as a conniving, backstabbing, spoiled little brat. Thanks to the show, we got to know him too well. And to know him is to Grrr! him.

And that's too bad.

The point is, if we didn't know anything about J. D. Fortune, we'd buy his records. We'd even make him a rock superstar. But we won't, even though INXS ultimately chose him as the winner of the competition and the new lead singer of the band—a poor decision, if you ask me.

Just imagine if the Allman Brothers' drug habits or personal clashes had been broadcast every Monday night on CBS, do you think we would have ever heard of "Rambling Man" or "Sweet Melissa"?

Of course not.

We consumers don't like to know what we're buying. Wrap it up in a pretty package and we're there. We don't really want to know how many trans fats there are, but since you told us, well, we don't want it anymore, no matter how good it tastes. Ignorance is bliss.

The same thing goes for our favorite artists. Too much information about an artist is never a good thing.

Why do you think Robert De Niro and Al Pacino don't do *MTV Cribs* or get *Punk'd*? They know better.

Whitney Houston's made enough money, so if her fans see her on her reality show *Being Bobby Brown* and decide they don't like Whitney the person, oh well. What does she care anymore?

But if Whitney were on a reality show first, she might have never achieved her "One Moment in Time" that made her the megastar she once was.

It's good to want to be successful. And if your success comes with fame and fortune, more power to you.

But just be careful how you get there, and don't reveal too much. We want mystery.

When singer J. D. Fortune won the *Rock Star* competition to become the lead singer of INXS, his claim to fame was a tune he wrote called "Pretty Vegas."

Today, that catchy tune can be heard on Top Forty and adult alternative rotations on both terrestrial and satellite radio several times a day.

But the song's catchiness isn't all it has going for it. It's a testament to Las Vegas casinos like, for instance, The Hard Rock.

The Hard Rock casino hotel can be described as both heaven and hell. One could easily take a look at all of the beautiful people around and say, "I think I've died and gone to heaven"—and two hours later look at all the money they lost and say, "I think I've died and gone to hell."

At poolside, muscled, toned, tattooed, and tanned bodies in the teeniest bikinis are in abundance. Young women with so-called tramp stamps (lower-back tattoos) and bleached blond hair sashay from the casino floor to poolside cabanas, where inevitably some guy signing $20,000 markers is picking up the tabs.

Waiters, waitresses, bartenders, and gaming staff are equally beautiful.

I watched a casting director from CBS's *Survivor* approach TJ, a beautiful blackjack dealer of Panamanian descent, and ask her if she would be interested in trying out for the show.

These days, Vegas, especially the Hard Rock, where celebrities hang out—Tom Brady and Nicky Hilton were there when I happened to be there "researching" this chapter,—is a place where dreams come true.

Heaven.

The new Vegas is one giant shopping mall with marble floors and vaulted ceilings, five-star restaurants and top-shelf liquor. It's where Cuban cigars aren't even the best you could buy (if they sold them) and beautiful people from Beverly Hills come to be seen and heard.

There's more sightseeing at poolside and inside the casinos then there is a few miles up the road in the beautiful Red Rock canyon.

After a while, however, the beautiful people melt away and become one giant mosaic of casino chips and paper money, makeup and silicone, JUICY rear ends, exotic perfumes, and rock 'n' roll music. It's all fun and games until somebody loses their shirt, but the pretense outweighs the risk.

This is the place to be seen and to see, worth the ebb and flow of the slots and the cards and the booze and the smoke.

Uptown on Fremont is the Vegas the mob built. Seedy and dangerous, where two-dollar tables do exist and gamblers eye one another with suspicion, but as one of my colleagues put it, there's something more honest about that part of town.

The old Vegas isn't hip and it ain't pretty, but at least you know where you stand, and the pace is slow enough for you to realize you just may not belong there.

On the strip, the distractions and the shows and the beautiful people will suck you in until you become part of the mosaic.

But hey, it's Vegas and it's fun. Just keep it all in perspective, and don't forget, "It ain't pretty."

Top Ten Ways To Spot Reality Oblivions

1. They hang out with losers who say things like, "Dude, when you were in *The Restaurant* . . ."

2. They show up on press lines at events that have absolutely nothing to do with them.

3. They have personal Web sites where they pitch themselves as motivational speakers. For a nominal fee of course.

4. They go on talk shows and say things like, "I'm pursuing hosting gigs and on-camera reporting positions," actually delusional enough to think they are qualified to appear on television where even one iota of credibility is required. (It used to be a Grrr! when former Miss Americas were hired as newscasters. These days that's an accomplishment of note).

5. They appear on MTV and VH1 shows about '80s hair bands as pop-culture experts.

6. They know what cow's intestines taste like.

7. They appear on celebrity editions of *Who Wants To Be a Millionaire,* playing for charity! Isn't that ironic? Aren't they the charity cases?

8. They are often seen haggling with the doorman of some trendy nightclub with lines like, "Don't you know who I am?"

9. Turn on the FOX Reality Channel.

10. They will do absolutely anything for their fifteen minutes of fame.

Grrr!

Steroid Nation:
Forget About Baseball,
We're *All* on 'Em

So Rafael Palmeiro and Barry Bonds were on steroids after all.

After testifying in front of Congress and all of America that he "never used steroids," Palmeiro was caught with his hand in the syringe jar.

Should that surprise you? It seems like everybody who wags his finger in denial in and around Washington sooner or later gets caught in a lie.

Bonds was outed by the book *Game Of Shadows,* and in spite of his attempts at lawsuits and his continuous silence on the issue, it seems America is convinced.

But the fact that the coulda-been Hall of Fame baseball players took steroids shouldn't surprise any of us.

After all, don't we live in a steroid nation? Think about it.

An SUV is a station wagon on steroids. A Hummer is an SUV on steroids. A mountain bike is a bicycle on steroids. PlayStation 2 is Atari on steroids. Cable TV is like your aerial antenna on steroids. DSL is your dial-up modem . . . on steroids.

We can go on and on. The truth of the matter—and this is not an excuse for steroid-using professionals—is we're all looking for anything that can increase performance, no matter what.

Your favorite Web site is probably cached on a content distribution network, like Akamai or Limelight. That means they're paying premium rates for bandwidth so that when you go to your favorite Internet page, you don't have to wait more than a few milliseconds for the page to load.

It's the Internet on steroids.

Men used to get their hair cut at barbershops. That wasn't good enough, so beauty salons now cater to men, charging tens of dollars more for a bad buzz cut. It's like your barber on steroids.

Malls are shopping centers . . . on steroids.

Twenty four-hour news channels are the evening news on steroids. Internet news sites are like newspapers on steroids.

For years, car manufacturers have looked for ways to increase performance, whether it's speed, acceleration, rack-and-pinion steering, better shocks, you name it. That wasn't enough, so after-market companies catering to performance-happy drivers sprang up everywhere. So we have after-market rims, after-market tires, after-market air intakes, spoilers, fins, super-chargers, you name it.

It's your car on steroids.

We will pay for performance. We pay extra for Amtrak's Acela service, because it's faster. For years, wealthy businessmen and women took the Concorde across the Atlantic, because it was faster.

Performance is king.

Steroids, both metaphorically and realistically, are a multi-billion-dollar industry.

We want faster horses. We want faster boats. We want bigger muscles. We want leaner, faster bodies and we want them now, without the work. Without the sacrifice. Give me a pill to make me live longer and I'll take it. Give me a pill to make me run faster and I'll take it. Give me a pill to make my body more desirable to me—whether that means taller, shorter, thinner, fatter—and I'll take it.

Not only are we taking it but one way or the other, we're willingly paying for it. If we didn't buy the superstar athlete, he wouldn't have to live up to synthetic expectations.

The point is, don't blame Palmiero or his baseball cohort Jason Giambi for taking steroids.

In fact, don't blame baseball players, football players, hockey players, wrestlers, track stars, or any athlete who pollutes his body in search of that competitive edge.

Isn't that what America is all about—having an edge?

I'm not saying it's right, but steroid use among athletes has gotten so out of control that the pros that don't take them are more than likely riding the bench. They're the ones nobody hears about. They're the ones nobody cares about and it's a Grrring shame.

Athletes who don't take steroids—both professional and amateur—will never be as good as the ones who do. And that means the sportswriters don't write about them, the TV cameras don't focus on them, and the gaming companies don't feature them.

It's always the hulking superstar athlete with the biggest locker, the biggest contract, the biggest agent, the covers of the hottest games and magazines, and the biggest needle—uh, competitive edge—getting all the accolades and setting new records.

It's a sad fact that at long last needs to be remedied.

Indeed, over the past few years, federal and local governments have worked hard to take away the illegal edge so many have enjoyed for so long, but athletes aren't the only ones looking for that extra edge.

The Martha Stewarts, Enrons, and Adelphias of the world learned the hard way that creative accounting or special treatment because of celebrity won't cut it anymore. Money was their edge.

The United Nations was embroiled in an Oil-for-Food scandal that involves Kofi Annan's son Kojo. Access to power was his edge.

Show business is full of people who are so beautiful they get paid tons of money just to show up.

Plastic surgery or other high-priced cosmetic procedures are likely their edge.

Ashlee Simpson and any number of pop tarts sell millions of CDs and bring in millions of dollars singing songs they don't write, and that don't even sound like them.

Technology in the studio is their edge.

Scott Peterson was found guilty by a jury of his peers. He thought a fancy, high-priced lawyer would be his edge. He thought wrong.

But before we blame any of them, before we cast stones in their direction, think about what you like to watch, what video games you like to play, what music you like to hear, and what you like your heroes to look like, act like, or play like.

Think about what you like to buy. Think about whose career you follow most closely. Think about whose picture you click on while surfing the Internet, what headline catches your eye, what sports highlight you watch over and over and over again.

Baseball fans, ask yourselves: Will you watch small ball? Will you watch a game where pitchers don't throw 98 miles per hour, where homers are fewer and where stars aren't rippling with muscles or burning around the bases? Will you pay big bucks to see athletes who look just like you?

I once asked Yankees manager Joe Torre about the controversy.

"When everything's said and done, I hope people still feel good about watching baseball," Torre said. "That's what we're here to do, to make baseball the sport it's supposed to be."

Good luck, coach. Until then all I can say is Grrrrrr!

THE FANATICS

Sport is a huge part of our culture. I love watching sports on television, although I do not go as far as a lot of people I know. Whenever he watched the Yankees on the tube, my brother-in-law Joe used to have to sit in his "lucky" chair while wearing the same pair of socks he wore the last time the Bronx Bombers won a game. Never mind that he grew up closer to the Phillies than the Yankees, but that's beside the point.

He was a nut about his sport fan superstitions. Now that he has two children, Gregory and Allie, with my sister, Melissa, he isn't so obsessive, which is a testament to how his priorities have changed. Thankfully.

But some people never grow up. Here are some sports Grrrs.

- Males over the age of sixteen should not wear football jerseys with their favorite player's name on it in public. It's just wrong to see adults wearing their Tiki jerseys at the game. Oh, I know, now you want to throw a beer on me or fight me about it, right? As an adult, wearing someone else's name on your shirt says a lot about how you feel about yourself, doesn't it? "Look guys, I may have been a terrible athlete myself, but I'm wearing Tiki Barber's jersey, so that makes me great." I don't really get it. For kids it's something to aspire to. For adults, it's cheesy.

- People who would stampede their own mother to get the free T-shirt that was shot into the stands, just because it's free. Grrr!

- Athletes are not gods. While their autographs on a ball could be worth money some day, the adoration these guys enjoy is oftentimes not even warranted. How many of these guys are steroid punks, anyway?

- Do they think the athlete they are screaming at can hear them from way up in those stands? Don't you just love those guys who carry on one-way conversations with their favorite or most hated players on the field? "Hey Pedro, you suck!" Yeah, and Pedro might reply, "And you're in the stands paying fifty bucks a seat to watch me suck."

- Alcohol should be banned at all arena events. It would save you a lot of money (ten dollars for a beer), and it would drastically reduce the number of Obliviot moments in the stands. And you just might be able to bring your children to the next home game. Imagine that.

▣ Watching the Super Bowl from nosebleed seats is hardly as entertaining as watching it from your living room. I've been there; trust me when I tell you, staying home is better.

"SOUNDS OF THE GAME"

Somebody's got to say it, so it might as well be the Grrr! Guy.

What is it with TV sports producers and their obsession with putting microphones on athletes for the "sounds of the game" or "miked-up" segments? Have any one of these athletes ever uttered anything that at least resembles the English language?

These segments, which usually feature a bunch of grunts or chest-pounding, don't come close to enhancing the viewer's experience.

It might be better if the athlete didn't know that what he was saying would be caught on tape. At least that way we as viewers might get a real insider's peek at what goes through the mind of a professional athlete. But noooo . . . that's not the case. Instead we are apparently to believe that "Blah blah whaa blah blah, that's what I'm talking 'bout" is a spontaneous statement and a daily game occurrence. Yeah, right.

Grrr! on these stupid segments which only serve the ego of an already overpaid athlete with an already inflated sense of self. I'd rather hear what the waterboy has to say.

Remember when football players used to look into the camera and say, "Hi, mom"? Nowadays when the camera comes near they turn into talking resumes. The NFL would be better off banning players from any on-camera time that isn't on the field of play, period.

BLING BLING

Grrr! to the term *bling!* Even better, Grrr! to the white talk-show hosts, the white sports reporters, and the white news anchors who use that term whenever they're interviewing a black celebrity or sports star.

"You've got some major bling on those earlobes." "You're sporting some bling-bling on that wrist."

First off, don't encourage the idiot man who's wearing two-carat diamond earrings in both his ears so he can show off how much disposable income he has.

Second, the term *bling* itself is stupid. It's ridiculous. And it's old.

And third—you look like a jackass when you try to endear yourself to whom you believe is your interviewee's demographic. Shut up and ask the same old vapid questions that some twenty-two-year-old "producer" making twenty-two grand a year wrote for you twenty-two minutes ago.

(((20)))

Television Worship: "Can You See Me?"

I'll admit that when I'm up late at night and I'm scrolling through the Guide on my cable system and notice a listing for a paid program on Spike TV, that I'll tune in because it's more than likely an infomercial for the latest *Girls Gone Wild* video.

How these clowns get these hot girls to flash the camera, make out with their girlfriends (or worse), and generally act like a bunch of whores for total strangers and ostensibly millions of masturbators is beyond me.

It's called Spring Break Fever. These kids think that while in Cabo San Lucas that anything goes and there's no harm. They can chalk it up to being young and experimental.

But where is the parental outrage? Can you imagine what it must be like for the father of one of these girls to flip through the channels and find his little angel in one of these videos performing some irresponsible sex acts with the college roommate she spent Spring Break with?

Holy cow!

It is however, extremely acceptable. I mean, it's on TV, isn't it? It must be okay. It's not really porn because these girls are just having fun, right? They're not professional strippers or adult video actresses. They're just girls having fun.

Of course, *Girls Gone Wild* is big business for the people behind the

DVDs. If these girls were smart they'd keep their boobs in their tank tops, at least until they were guaranteed payment for revealing their assets. But that will never happen, because these are girls who want to be seen. They want to be on television. And who doesn't? You're nobody in this country until somebody sees you on TV.

Why else do you think people make complete Obliviots out of themselves whenever a camera is turned in their direction? Very well-educated men turn into ignorant morons when a camera, particularly at sporting events, focuses on them. They point their fingers in the air and scream, "We're number one!" to nobody in particular.

Stand in Times Square when MTV's broadcasting *Total Request Live.* Hundreds of teenagers are lined up on the street, just waiting for their cue to look up at the camera and yell and scream like idiots.

Walk the streets with a camera and a microphone, and people will have an opinion on places they've never been or people they've never met. One time I was covering a Spring Break in Fort Lauderdale. There I was on the beach walking with a camera crew and a microphone in my hand, when a woman with two young daughters came running up to me. "Can my girls be on television?"

These girls were like eleven and twelve, but I didn't have the heart to tell her no, so I asked some innocuous questions that would never make the piece. When I was done "interviewing" the girls, Mom asked, "Where can we see this?"

"Girls Gone Wild," was my answer. She freaked out a bit before I told her I was just kidding. But I pointed out to her that next time she saw a camera crew walking on the beach during Spring Break, or anywhere for that matter, she might not want to be so forthcoming with her daughters, because these days you never know where that image will be shown.

DO YOU SEE ME?

The people sitting behind home plate at World Series games are even worse, albeit with their clothes on. They spend the whole time with their cell phones glued to their ears, talking with everyone they ever knew.

"Do you see me now?"

Gee, it's a good thing you called to tell me that was you with the ridiculous cowboy hat on at the Yankees-Angels game. And all this time I thought you were dead.

Do you even like baseball?

Never mind. You've got bucks. You don't need fans at the big games. They can't afford tickets anyway. World Series and Super Bowl tickets are extremely overpriced, but then again, for those spectacular events the best seat in the house will always be in your living room.

And if you have a High Definition television, more power to you. I bought an HDTV and I'll be hard-pressed to ever attend a live event again. Who needs $500 courtside seats when you've got HDTV?

And lucky me can see the Obliviot in the background with the cell phone to his ear, waving frantically everytime there's a shot of home plate. I can see him more clearly now, too, and yup, I was right. He *is* an idiot.

YOU'RE NOBODY UNTIL YOU'RE ON TV

It's a bit hypocritical coming from a guy who makes his living in the broadcast industry, but the notion that you're nobody until you're on television is ludicrous.

But the things that make people famous these days are so ass-backwards that it is really true that there's no such thing as bad publicity. Paris Hilton makes a porn video and she becomes a household name. Go figure. As far as amateur porn goes, Hilton has nothing on Pam Anderson and Tommy Lee, but they were already famous and already didn't care what people thought of them, so it didn't matter. Besides, did you see that tape?

But today anything goes, because there are so many choices for viewers to choose from—Internet, hundreds of channels—that the execs who put people on TV are going for the quick bang rather than the tried-and-true.

Plus, picking programs has gotten as bad as picking stocks on Wall Street.

The Monkey Index (where an actual monkey picks stocks) does better than the Standard and Poor Index some years. These days a hit reality show is watching singer Lisa Loeb try to find a boyfriend. At least she's better-looking than Ozzy Osbourne and his kids—but then again, so are Hugh Hefner's *Girls Next Door,* and I wouldn't be caught dead watching that show.

The result of all of this bad TV is that instead of producing high-quality shows with talented hosts, writers, and producers, what we have are things airing on networks that were once products of college or high school TV production classes, or YouTube.

It's not good enough, no matter how much money they bring in. What's next? Actually airing Tommy & Pam's sex tape and others like it?

Where's the integrity?

You're an Oblivion If . . .

o You drop your cigarette butts anywhere you wish.

o You e-mail me to complain about people who complain.

o You wait until the last minute to whip out the checkbook or count your quarters at the checkout line (see also *Wal-Martians*.)

o You cut in front of people who are waiting in line because your tunnel vision only allows you to see what you need at any particular moment in time.

o You block the cereal aisle with your cart as you debate the pros and cons of Chex Mix versus Frosted Mini Wheats with your kids.

Grrr!

21

Polignorants and Other Beltway Grrr!s

Remember the "War on Christmas"? It became a liberal versus conservative war, a Democrat versus Republican debate.

What a bunch of hogwash.

What, do all conservative-minded Americans necessarily practice the Christian faith? There are no Jewish conservatives or atheist conservatives or Muslim conservatives? Do no liberals worship Christ? There is not one Christmas tree among them? Are all liberals secularists? Please, people.

But that was just the latest example of how ridiculous we've become in our collective us-vs.-them attitude. At a time when the holidays are supposed to unite us all, we're looking for even more ways to polarize our nation.

In one of my columns I Grrred Victoria's Secret for making a bra worth some $12.5 million, quoting Giselle Bundchen's remark about how that money could feed a country. One reader responded by asking how many countries the Bush Administration could feed with what the war on terror costs, adding that I'm a right-wing nutjob.

Huh? How do you equate the cost of a diamond-encrusted bra that no woman in her right mind would wear to the cost of fighting a war against terrorists?

It's just somebody looking for anything to politicize.

In response to that same column, I was chastised via e-mail with accusations like "Liberals and African Americans on your list: poor form" and "Come on, who do you work for, CNN, you liberal piece of garbage?"

You see? In a column where actors and a few athletes made my "Oblivions of 2005" roundup, someone goes and puts social labels on them. (At least my label is made up.) Because I included a well-known Republican ("Scooter" Libby), I'm a "liberal piece of garbage."

Perhaps I should write a column about my favorite flavor of ice cream and see which side of the aisle sends me the most hate mail.

I can picture it now: "It's no wonder you like vanilla ice cream because George Bush doesn't care about black people," or "Of course you like vanilla ice cream, because you're soft. I bet you liked *Brokeback Mountain*, too, and support gay marriage, you liberal faggot."

You probably think I'm kidding. I'm not.

Far too many of us in this country are going to extreme lengths to find anything to disagree about politically.

But it's not only the people on the far side of either aisle.

If you're at all conservative, try reading Frank Rich's column that is ostensibly about entertainment, and you won't be able to read it all the way through before dropping the paper in anger, and if you're a liberal, just try listening to AM radio for more than ten minutes and you'll be ordering up satellite radio for those endless road trips before long.

The truth of the matter is, we are more and more living in a political maelstrom. There's a perfect storm brewing, and if we choose to continue sailing these seas, we're going to be in for a longer, rougher voyage than the one we've already embarked on.

PROTESTORS FROM HELL

I thought long and hard about including this Grrr! in the book, because I took a lot of heat by the liberals who will protest just about anything under the sun for the sake of demonstrating.

That's not to say protesting a war is not a worthy cause.

But demonstrators discredit their cause and themselves when they show up unwashed, acting unruly, and smoking pot in the middle of Washington, D.C.

Let me explain my weekend from hell in our nation's capital, where stem cell research advocates to Cindy Sheehan sympathizers, protestors of all shapes, sizes, colors, and odors gathered for a cause.

Unfortunately for me—since I was traveling by train—a whole lot of them originated from or passed through New York's Penn Station, and a train delay made matters worse.

A steel girder collapsed on the tracks just outside the station, and it was just what the doctor ordered for a bunch of anxious, ready-to-protest-just-about-anything Obliviots—err, demonstrators—who gathered with their anti-Bush cardboard signs and their 1967-era wardrobes.

As if the tie-dyed clothes weren't stereotypically Grrring enough, they just couldn't help but break into song.

Yup. You guessed it. "All we are saying, is give peace a chance." Yeah, all I'm saying is get a grip and get a new song. Do these morons think they're being original?

A lot of these people would join a rally against Dr. Seuss if Sam I Am actually ate his green eggs and ham earlier in the book. I'm actually surprised PETA hasn't called for a widespread burning of the popular children's tome.

Of course, the right to demonstrate against one's government is the mark of a true democracy. Unfortunately for my nasal passages and sense of smell, most of the demonstrators feel that the mark of a true democracy is the right not to bathe.

At lunch at D.C.'s Union Station I was treated to more anti-Bush fodder from a trio of demonstrators who appeared not to have taken showers for at least three months.

What is it about protestors and poor hygiene? Maybe they double as antiwar and prowater conservationists?

If I thought that these Oblivions were Grrring on the way down to D.C., I was treated to a return trip to New York on a train loaded with a bunch of now sweaty, loud, and even smellier protestors who recounted to each other the day's events. Lucky me.

One complete Obliviot—who splayed out her bare feet on the empty seat next to her (no wonder it was empty)—watched her camcorder with full audio of the day's protests.

Apparently, someone who was in the general vicinity of her camera had one of those siren bullhorns you hear at high school football games, and I was forced to listen to its wail for the majority of the ride home.

The nineteen-year-old behind me talked on her cell phone with her obviously disapproving parents and she argued relentlessly why she had the right to waste her time and travel to D.C. for a "good cause."

"Why is it every time I talk with you we get into an argument. You know, Joan Baez was there. Isn't she your age? Hello? Hello?"

The woman with the camcorder and the bare feet was now flossing her teeth. I kid you not.

She had a long thread of floss hanging down from her mouth and her hands were going back and forth. Yup, she then spit on the Amtrak floor. Your proud protestors, ladies and gentlemen. Thankfully I let my cameraman go before I made this trip. You're spared.

The person in front of me was eating the most foul-smelling Chinese food. Why do people insist on eating odiferous foods in public places like trains? You've got to be kidding me. These people are complete Oblivions, but hey, who am I to protest their right to free assembly?

They think they're making a difference?

All they were doing was causing a ruckus in places that don't matter. Penn Station? Union Station? Yeah, sing to your heart's content, you're wasting your time.

Okay, now someone was singing protest songs, and boy, the Barry Gibb falsetto complete with shaky notes was really beautiful. I mean, sign me up to your cause right now!

Oooh, yum. The Chinese food odor was making me really hungry for some grotesque-smelling MSG. Do you think they'll deliver if I call ahead to the next stop? Maybe I'll order something with extra garlic.

Awww, now the nineteen-year-old was crying, saying "I love you, I love you, can you hear me? I love you Daddy." Touching, really. She appeared to be drunk out of her mind, by the way. Not that I couldn't have used a stiff Johnny Walker Black right about then. "Hello? Hello?" Why couldn't she understand that cell service wasn't so good on the train line from Washington to points north?

These demonstrators were the kind of people who force otherwise pleasant Amtrak employees to make announcements like, "In case you haven't noticed, this is a sold-out train. Therefore remove your items, your bare feet, your picket signs, your papers, laptops, jackets, and everything else from the seat next to you. If you don't, we will be happy to charge you for the extra seat."

More singing from two seats behind me. I couldn't contain myself. If only I were an A&R executive from Virgin Records, I'd have the next Barry Gibb signed up by the time I reached Philadelphia. Joan who?

You know, after such a touching display of human nature from the protestors, I might have to call on the president to pull all our troops out of Iraq. I mean, surely the good folks on this train would much rather have Iraq fend for itself right about now.

Hey look, I just happened to be on the antiwar protest line. There were a few hundred prowar demonstrators as well, and I bet their train home was equally amusing. Next time I'll be sure to get on that line to Grrr! that bunch, too, although I bet their train was heading to points south.

THE MAN'S KEEPING ME DOWN!

Let's play the blame game.

Rep. Cynthia McKinney (D-Ga.) blamed racism after she was stopped by a white Capitol police officer because he didn't recognize her.

Remember the story of how McKinney was entering the Longworth building when she breezed past a metal detector? When McKinney ignored calls from the officer for her to stop and show identification, she then turned and allegedly struck him after he grabbed her wrist.

Sounds like racism to me. Yup. And I know about racism.

Just the other day, I was stopped by a FOX security guard because my identification was not visible as I entered one of the rooms that is staffed with a guard. These are doors that I pass through every day, and the guard knows I pass every day.

But he has a job to do, so I showed him my identification. What's the big deal?

Do you think he stopped me because I have olive skin? After all, my mother is from Chile, even though I look like someone out of an episode of *The Sopranos*, and I do speak semifluent Spanish.

Surely that qualifies as a case of Latin profiling, no?

Look, we all know there is racism in this country and that we still have a long way to go in that area. If you don't believe me, just watch the Oscar-winning movie *Crash*.

What is so poignant about the movie is that every character who believes he is a victim of racism harbors his own racist views toward the people he believes harbor racist views toward him.

In short, it takes a racist to know a racist.

McKinney held a press conference in which she got no support from any other members of Congress—black, white, Republican, or Democrat. She was, however, accompanied by two noted civil rights leaders, the singer Harry "Come Mr. Tallyman tally me bananas" Belafonte, and Danny "Lethal Weapon" Glover.

I will be holding my own press conference about my Latin blood profiling at a later date, and I've got calls in to Reese Witherspoon, Salma Hayek, and Charlize Theron to join me.

What do they have to do with my plight? Well, nothing, really. I just thought it would be a good opportunity for them to get face time for a national cause, and for me to get some face time with them.

Once they agree to attend, you can bet that the building security guards will shudder at my Hollywood support, and they'll agree to settle for millions of dollars for me to go away.

What a country!

HILLARY CLINTON ON ENTITLEMENT

There was a time that I was beginning to wonder if Senator Hillary Rodham Clinton was about to switch from Democrat to Republican.

When she came down hard on Generation Y in the summer of 2006 with comments to the effect that young people today have a feeling of entitlement when it comes to the workforce, I couldn't help but agree.

The liberal bloggers were all up in arms about it because she sounded like a conservative (gasp!) but I couldn't give a Grrr! about them. And for all of you ultraconservative Clinton haters, please don't give me any "Chelsea Clinton makes six figures as a consultant" bullshit, either. Chelsea Clinton has done some extraordinary things in her young life, and no matter what your politics, you can't take that away from her.

Nobody has ever accused Chelsea Clinton of not pulling her weight.

The simple, sad truth is kids these days think that a college degree is tantamount to a $75,000-a-year job. They also believe that an internship is a guarantee of future employment once said intern receives his or her diploma.

I've seen this firsthand.

A former intern of mine once asked me to have lunch with her and proceeded to argue with me and pout (seriously) about why she hasn't been hired at some television network.

There was no reasoning with her.

The fact that it wasn't yet two weeks since she'd graduated wouldn't assuage her sense of entitlement.

Also, when I asked her what she wanted to do, she couldn't grasp the fact that "I only want to work in entertainment" seriously limited her prospects in New York City, a predominately hard-news town—at least when it comes to entry-level positions at the networks.

My advice to her was to either move to Los Angeles or reconsider her job requirements. Needless to say, that lunch ended badly when I told her there was nothing more I could do to help her.

Now, there are certain industries that may reward the slackers and the what-about-mes. How many of you work with people who don't work a second past eight hours without putting in for overtime or a comp day, or who berate the boss day in and day out for a pay raise—and then get it?

Of course, it is not only Generation Y that is guilty of feeling entitled, and it is a false generalization to state that all young adults feel like they don't need to work hard to get ahead.

There are very many hard-working kids entering the workforce. There are also many lazy, good-for-nothing, negative whiners who have been toiling away for years with the attitude that the world is against them.

I feel for the families of those types of people. What kind of an example must they be setting for their kids?

In my experience, the hard workers are not necessarily the products of great schools, great GPAs, or great internships. For the most part, hard workers are the products of great parents or the positive influence of some adult way back in an individual's developing years.

That said, there are also individuals who don't want to end up like their parents and subsequently work hard to get out.

Whenever I ask someone I'm impressed with where they get their drive, they usually tell me a story about a childhood experience that taught them that hard work is the only way to get ahead.

Inspiration is hard to put your finger on.

It could come in the shape of a book. Biographies of famous people, business leaders, or educators might be what you need to help you strive for your goal. It could be movie like *Rudy* or even *Working Girl,* or it could be your mother or father, a boss, a coworker, or a coach who inspires you.

The bottom line is, nobody deserves anything. Not until we've earned it.

An Open Letter to an Oblivion

Dear Oblivion,

I trust this letter finds you well, although since the world revolves around you, there's probably not much getting in your way.

Contrary to popular belief among your ranks, there are other people in the world.

Believe it or not, you are no more special than the rest of us who wait on line for our tickets, our coffee, or at the highway exit. Therefore, blasting by us in the through traffic lane and then cutting off the person at the front of the exit is generally rude behavior, not to mention bad driving etiquette.

But *etiquette* is a word not in the Oblivion vocabulary.

Etiquette would dictate that you don't yell into your cell phone so that the person on the other end of the call doesn't have to scramble to turn the volume down, and the people next to you at the restaurant don't have to hear your lame conversation.

Etiquette would also dictate that you don't smuggle a bag of potato chips into "*The Dukes of Hazzard*" and proceed to crinkle the bag and munch to your heart's content in the middle of the theater.

Speaking of the theater, they post the showtimes for a reason.

Arriving after a movie begins and then having the audacity to demand that people fill in the empty seats in the middle of a row so you and your Obliviot pal can sit together is beyond reason.

Grrr!

Then again, reason is another thing Oblivions can't quite comprehend.

Reason would require sensitivity to another person's point of view or behaving in a manner reasonable to society. For instance, staring down a retail clerk who is busy helping another customer or interrupting that clerk while he or she is busy with said previous customer and demanding attention is beyond reason.

And hear this: Even if all you have is a "quick question," it doesn't mean that it's okay for you to skip all the unwritten rules that make up a civilized experience.

Some of those unwritten rules include, but are not limited to:

o Waiting patiently for one's turn in a line.

o Treating service personnel with respect and even tipping when customary.

o Keeping to the right when traveling at slow speeds (both while driving and walking).

o Moving away from the bottom of an escalator after stepping off the mechanism.

o Waiting to board an elevator or a subway train until everybody who is deboarding has done so.

o Chewing gum or other foods with your mouth closed—thus sparing people around you the grotesque sound of your saliva smacking around your food and mouth.

22

Stupid Lit'l Dreamer

Living the American Dream means living in a pressure cooker.

We all want to provide for our families, and that means a nice house with a nice TV (premium cable package, of course), heating in the winter and air-conditioning in the summer, and a respectable set of wheels to get us to the grocery store, where generic brands don't even exist anymore.

And there's nothing wrong with any of that.

We go to work, and even if we make a decent living, or more than our parents did when they were our age, we're still struggling to make ends meet, and you have to wonder just how did Mom and Dad pull it off.

Whether that's a product of our hyperconsumerism or simply the rising cost of living year after year doesn't matter. It's simply a fact of life.

And then you see the latest Chase bank commercial.

It's shot on black-and-white film and plays out against a cover tune of Bette Midler's "Wind Beneath My Wings" from the tearjerker *Beaches*.

And even in a commercial, the song does its due, and before you know it you're blubbering like Robert De Niro's gangster-in-therapy character from *Analyze This*.

The commercial is about a man paying for his daughter's wedding, with clever flashbacks to tender moments between a little girl and her father, intercut with the old man escorting his pride and joy down the aisle into the arms of her fiancé, then writing a check to the caterer at the end of the reception.

The message is: Chase Manhattan Bank is there to help you plan for these moments.

Yeah, it's a tearjerker, but it's also enough to make any young parent become stricken with fear and pressure to be *that* guy in the commercial. And then the reality of how much money you owe hits you like a sledgehammer over the head.

You run to the computer and log in to the company 401(k) Web site to check your retirement fund or your personal savings account, where the "amount you owe" column seems to be growing as the "credit" column seems to be diminishing.

Funny how that happens, isn't it?

But we tell ourselves it will all be okay. Something will happen. We'll get out from under. We'll step in something that will mean a change in our way of life—something better for our family.

With that bit of self-reassurance (or denial) helping you feel a little better, you begin to channel-surf through the premium cable package and land on Anthony Bourdain's *No Reservations* on the Travel Channel.

Bourdain is the former New York City chef who wrote the best-selling book *Kitchen Confidential,* which later became the basis for a FOX TV show.

Just when you're done freaking out over the Chase commercial and your seemingly imminent Chapter 7 bankruptcy filing, Bourdain says on his show, "I was a guy with a regular job as a chef, sweating behind the lines of restaurants for twenty years, and then I write one over-the-top, obnoxious book and my life changes overnight."

Aha! Hope.

These days, Bourdain spends his time traveling the world for national television, tasting the finest wines and gourmet foods from some of the most exotic or simplest places on Earth, and he watched history unfold before his eyes when, while shooting in Beirut, war with Israel erupted.

His life went from being a grunt behind the kitchen lines of rat-infested cockroach havens otherwise known as overpriced, hoity-toity four- and five-star restaurants (where his life looked enviable only to the ditchdigger who worked the overnight shift in the state highway maintenance department), to being the bon vivant who gets paid to live a life of luxury, where his life is envy-inspiring.

Bourdain is a new millennium version of LeRoy Neiman's "man about town."

All in all, not a bad way to live. Bourdain is an example of one form of the American Dream. Another version is the guy in the Chase commercial—the hero—the wind beneath his childrens' wings who can provide for them and make a life for them.

The challenge we face is having a little bit of both—a balance of Bourdain's worry-free wanderer and the Chase commercial guy's confident caretaker.

That's the American Dream. The Grrr! is a way to help deal with the journey.

Keep Grrring, and keep dreaming.

STEPPING UP

There is incompetence everywhere.

Recently I heard two versions as to why someone couldn't correct a problem coming out of his department. One was he didn't have electricity in his apartment, so he was unable to log on to the office network. The second was he didn't get the page because he was in the subway.

Two very different excuses generating the same result: the problem didn't get fixed as quickly as it should have.

The bottom line is: rare is the person willing to be held accountable for their incompetence or their actions.

So where does the problem stem from? I think it's pretty easy to identify. Kids who get poor test scores these days can point to their teachers. After all, if the teachers taught better, the scores would be higher, right?

Violent criminals can point to the big bad make-believe violence on television, in video games, and at the movies. After all, nobody has violent thoughts until they are exposed to graphic images on some screen, right?

And of course, according to conservative think tank Rand Corp, teenagers are having premarital sex only because they are exposed to sexy ads in magazines, music videos starring beautiful people gyrating suggestively and the proliferation of pornography. God knows nobody would even think of sex before marriage without those outside stimulants.

Underperforming employees say they are overworked or underpaid. They say they don't have enough resources allocated to get the job done. They say there are not enough hours in the day or that the battery in their pager was dead when they were needed. Somehow it's the company's fault that the batteries they provide for the pagers don't simply last forever. It's never about them.

No. Sorry. Ain't gonna work.

Where does society's role in shaping general behavior begin and end? It's easy to blame the big companies that make money peddling substandard morals. But who sets those standards? We live in a free country. Just as one man's trash is another man's treasure, one person's favorite song or show can be another person's source of revulsion.

The solution to so many of our societal issues lies within us, and only we truly know what our individual strengths are.

Do you have what it takes to commit to a job where an employer is paying you to perform tasks? If not, please quit and open up the slot for someone who does.

Do you have what it takes to be a father or a mother, where your role is most important?

If not, please don't have kids. In a country where one needs a license for just about everything, where home economics and typing are courses in high school, it amazes me that there are no licenses required to have children or, at the very least, no mandatory courses in basic child rearing in high school or college. No, of course somebody would be offended.

Plus, teachers don't know anything, remember? If they did, whom would we blame for our shortcomings?

We live in a society where money is king, where fame is enviable, and where getting into a hot club or wearing the right pair of jeans at any cost is really, really important.

If you could come up with a list of your top desires, where would "doing the right thing" fall on that list?

Doing the right thing barely makes the top five of our desires. If you want to change the world, you have to start with you. If we all do that, we'd all be much happier, and good times and a sensible society become inevitable.

But what is it about our culture that promotes mediocrity?

Very few industries today are singled out for promoting people based on merit. Very few executives, pop stars, actors, or journalists deserve to be where they are today.

The thing about this life is, somebody has to say yes.

No matter how good you are, somebody in a position of power has to say yes.

No matter how much you want something or how dedicated you are to something, that yes is out of your hands.

It's as simple as that.

If you watch TV on a regular basis, you probably know you could read a teleprompter better than many of the anchors you're watching. You probably know that the spokesperson on your favorite cable news channel who happens to be talking about the industry you work in really doesn't understand it any better than you do.

You probably know more about sports than the guy on ESPN or on your local television station.

You're probably smarter than most of the people who attend the college you had your heart set on but couldn't get into.

If you listen to music, or if you attend a live concert where some megabucks pop star is lip-synching because she can't sing nearly as well as the music companies would have you believe, you might be thinking you can do it better.

If there's one thing *American Idol* has demonstrated, good singers don't have to hide behind the technology of a sound studio or the tricks of producers.

Models are airbrushed. Radio voices are filtered. Sports stars are professionally trained using state-of-the-art equipment or, worse, performance-enhancing drugs. Actors do dozens of takes of the same scene until they get it right. Your boss is taking credit for your work, and her boss is taking credit for her work, and so on.

The dichotomy here is that for most people, getting to that yes takes so much sweat equity that after finally obtaining it, they'll do as little as possible to set themselves apart from the pack.

They figure, "Finally, I can coast." And they do. It's bittersweet, isn't it? But nobody's doing anything about it.

Why?

Because the few people who are awarded that yes based on merit are too busy doing.

They are so busy tending to the task at hand that the coasters below them can skate along unnoticed. The truly successful people are too busy being successful to recognize the incompetence around them.

Overachievers know that they can make up for the slackers, so they do.

And that leaves the hard workers to fend for themselves and to claw their way up. It forces them to find innovative ways around the people in their way. It forces them to create their own opportunities.

Someone really smart once said that "luck is what happens when preparation meets opportunity."

That's not a bad way of looking at things. So stay prepared. Don't give up hope, but at the same time don't just hope.

You have to do something about whatever it is that's making you sick in your career. It really is up to you. Tell yourself yes, and the guy with the green light will have no choice but to follow your lead.

MY MEAN BOSS

As if being an overweight child isn't bad enough, a study in *Pediatrics* magazine once showed that overweight children are subject to more bullying on the playground than normal-weight kids are.

Hello? We needed an expensive study to figure that out? I could have told you that. Next time make the check out to Mike Straka, S-T-R-A-K-A.

All fat kids should be required to take martial-arts lessons. Not only will it get them in better shape, but when some bully decides to pick on them, they can kick his butt all over the playground, too.

I'm talking boys *and* girls. There's no rule anywhere that says catty girls shouldn't get their butts kicked by the girl they're picking on.

And *no*, I don't condone kids fighting anywhere that there isn't a mat and a referee, but there comes a time when kids should be toughened up rather than coddled.

Wake up, parents. Stop being complacent with your children. It's okay to demonstrate a little disappointment and offer encouragement, but don't be competitive with your children. You had your chance.

Nothing Grrrs me more than when I see some dad or mom talking to their children about how much better he or she did it at the children's ages. Stop living in the past and let your children live in their present.

If your kid is getting bullied because he's fat, short, skinny, or tall, help him find something constructive in it.

It kind of reminds me of my first mean boss, Larry. He was a news director, where I worked the overnight shift (1:00 A.M.–9:00 A.M.) as a desk assistant.

Whenever he walked into the newsroom, a chilly breeze would follow him into his office. Nobody was exempt from his wrath. From desk assistants to famous anchors, all persons were equally susceptible to a humiliating tongue-lashing.

But you know what? If I'm good in a newsroom, I have that man to thank.

If you didn't like being belittled, then you needed to know your job. You needed to know what was going on. You needed to react to breaking news like it was second nature. You needed to keep everybody abreast on developments with clarity. In short, he toughened me up.

I remember one instance when I was chasing a breaking news story. I was making calls to a hospital where a story was developing, and since several media outlets were also calling the hospital, the person answering the phone told me they were not taking any more calls from media outlets and asked that we stop calling.

In a note I put out to the newsroom I wrote, "The hospital told me to take a hike."

Larry came bursting out of his office.

"Mike, Mike," he always repeated my name whenever he was about to yell. "What did they say?" he asked. I told him the hospital spokesperson said they weren't talking to the media anymore.

"Then that's what you write. I don't want any of your stylistic bull———," he screamed. I said that I understood, but I really thought he was just being a big jerk.

When I finally got it, some time after that incident, I completely understood. He wasn't yelling for the sake of yelling.

I sent that note out to the entire newsroom. Some anchor could have taken my note for what it said, and it could very well have made it on the air that "So and So Hospital told us to take a hike," and it would have been wrong.

The point is, sometimes a little bullying goes a long way to help one's maturity, and there's always a lesson in it, even if it hurts. Stop whining and start learning.

LOOKING FOR PACINO

Al Pacino looks me directly in the eye when he talks to me.

Of course, it doesn't hurt that he and I are about the same height. Or both lack height, that is. We both stand around five feet, six inches. That, sadly for me, is where the similarity ends.

When I was acting in *Tony n' Tina's Wedding* in New York City several years ago, a few of my fellow castmates and I tossed around ideas for a movie we were going to make called *Looking for Pacino*.

Named loosely for the Pacino-directed *Looking for Richard*, it was about three unemployed actors so obsessed with their favorite screen star, each would take on the persona of their favorite Pacino character and then stalk the real Pacino.

I was always Michael Corleone of *The Godfather*, Pat was Tony Montana of *Scarface*, and Rocco was Vincent Hanna, the gritty cop in the Pacino/Robert De Niro flick, *Heat*.

"You straightened my brother out?" "You Cock-a-roash." "Gimme all you got!"

You get the idea.

We never did write that movie, and like so many other faces come and gone, I never really saw much of those guys after ending my run in the play. But I did get to meet Pacino twice, while covering the Tribeca Film Festival.

What struck me most about the legendary actor is how giving he is.

Even as festival cofounder De Niro dashes up the red carpet with barely a wave, Pacino stops at every camera, every microphone, every notepad. If not for his publicist, he might still be out there.

"Get me in front of the cameras and I can't stop," Pacino says apologetically, as his publicist pulls him away. He was about to be late for a Q&A session at a festival screening of his latest self-directed film, *Chinese Coffee,* starring Pacino and the late *Law and Order* star Jerry Orbach.

After the film, a woman from the audience approached a microphone to talk to Pacino, who sat onstage under a blue spotlight taking questions. Her body shook as she tried to say something. Eventually the words came out of her mouth as quickly as the tears streamed down her face.

"It was so incredible. Thank you," she said. Pacino smiled broadly, and with that creased face and those sharp green eyes we've all seen so many times on the silver screen, he embraced her.

"I'm glad I'm not alone, because it [the piece] had the same effect on me the first time I saw it at the Actor's Studio," he said. The rest of the Q&A had a similar give and take, as would any theater filled with Corleones, Montanas, and Hannas.

It's not surprising then, that Pacino was voted the greatest actor of all time in a 2003 United Kingdom poll. His *Heat* and *Godfather, Part II* costar, De Niro, was voted number two.

Recalling the year Pacino and De Niro presented a Best Picture Oscar together, I asked him if he, too, felt the Earth move the way I do, whenever he and De Niro are in the same room.

"I never really thought about it," he said. "I've known Bobby since he was this big," gesturing a small boy. "Bob's a great artist, and a great fellow," he added, noting the Tribeca Film Festival and all it stands for, with its mission of reviving the lower Manhattan spirit and economy after September 11.

The TFF is a force to be reckoned with, boasting film entries from all over the world, a giant family street festival, an MTV-sponsored concert and some of the world's biggest stars.

Pacino, a native New Yorker, wouldn't be anywhere else. In his final words of the evening, he gave some inspiration to the crowd full of aspiring filmmakers, actors, and fans.

"What you have to do is find a way to make it for yourself," he said.

"Despite all the obstacles and all the people saying you can't do it—you *can* find a way if you truly have something to say."

Actors, for the most part, usually have something to say. De Niro is unique among them, because inexplicably, he shuns the media spotlight. Friends say he's shy, although he's probably seen his share of love and hate from members of the entertainment press, and keeps his distance in order to keep his sanity.

Take A. O. Scott's article in *The New York Times*. In an April 20, 2003 piece titled "Seen This Guy Lately?" about De Niro's pal Pacino, Scott praises Pacino in a backhanded sort of way.

"His [Pacino's] reputation as one of our finest actors survives in spite of the mediocrity of so many of his projects," Scott wrote. He goes on to dissect and analyze Pacino the actor and Pacino the person.

What film critics like Scott, and his former *Times* colleague Elvis Mitchell, don't quite get is that the average filmgoer doesn't take movies as seriously as they do. Being a film critic, however, *is* serious business. After all, it puts food on their tables, and their love for words and essay structure is something to be cherished, particularly Mitchell's, albeit with a dictionary close by.

For most of us, though, a movie is just a movie. It's an event we go to to help take our minds off of the reality of our own lives and the world around us. Rarely do today's mainstream films speak to social conditions as effectively as they did in the early days of the medium.

Hollywood movies, for the most part, are pure entertainment. But that's not really a bad thing. In them we find reasons to make them our own, like the words to our favorite songs.

When I was a wrestler in high school it was a movie called *Vision Quest* that inspired me to take to the mat, much like *The Insider* inspires the TV news producer in me today. And I can watch them over and over again whenever the need to relive the glory days arises, or to help reinvigorate what I do today.

Movies are so much more than their box-office receipts. They are more than the nuances of filmmaking or the motivation of their origins, and more than just their reviews.

They inspire. They distract. They entertain. And that's why movies are important.

Pacino is one of the ambassadors to our dreams. Thanks, Al. If only more of your Hollywood colleagues would observe and imitate you, on screen and off.

23

A Grrr!-jestic Interlude: Some Non-Grrrs

The "Grrr!" column can have it's moments of nonjadedness, however infrequent they may be. Here are a few columns that struck a chord.

FORGIVENESS

This "Grrr!" column is about forgiveness

I know it's easier to say than to do, but as terrorists are busy blowing up innocent civilians who pay their taxes, work hard to provide for their families, thrive on freedom and love their fellow men, it's time to look at the person who has hurt you the most in your life—and forgive them their trespass against you.

I'm not talking about the lower-than-life terrorists here. They can burn in hell for all I care. And I'm not talking about the Oblivions who are the source of daily Grrrs—they'll never go away.

I'm talking about the husband or wife whose eye wandered too far one night. I'm talking about the father or mother who disowned their child because they married the "wrong" person or have the "wrong" political or religious beliefs. I'm talking about sisters and brothers and the college roommates who haven't spoken to each other for years and can't even remember why.

It's high time we remember where we came from and who helped us get from there to here.

Each and every one of us in America is lucky to be in a country where freedom is a given.

Sure, things aren't always grand. We question our leadership at times. We question our lives' paths at times. But at least we have the freedom to choose those paths.

And right now, the path to healing whatever ails you is to forgive, and to love your family, your closest friends, your coworkers and your neighbors.

With that choice you will find peace within. It's really that simple.

You can even start this process by focusing on the thing that worries you the most.

Is it credit card debt that keeps you up at night? Believe it or not, financial freedom will do wonders for your health.

Is it the bottle of wine that you can't seem to avoid? Cutting down on alcohol, and on eating for the sake of eating, will not only help you feel better physically, it will also help you feel better about yourself.

I don't mean to sound preachy, but I noticed recently that most of the problems I have with my life have to do with me, and only me. I can choose to love unconditionally, or I can choose to nitpick all the way to my grave.

I choose the former from now on.

But that doesn't mean I'll stop Grrring the little things that drive us nuts day in and day out. The little things are fun.

It's the big things that are hard to deal with and that need the most attention.

Striving for anything beyond the realm of the ordinary will put you in a gray area where some people are inspired by you and others will do whatever they can to keep you down.

When encountering the former, it would be best to encourage them to follow their own dreams with hard work and integrity. When encountering the latter, it's best to ignore them.

Negative people will set you back in your career and in your life.

When you believe in yourself, anything is possible.

But what gives you the strength to face that energy and win?

It could be the pride you put in your career. It could be the proud home you've made with your spouse. It could be your faith, or it could be the look on your little girl's face as she runs to greet Daddy or Mommy when you walk through the door at the end of the day.

It could be all of the above.

Whatever it is that gives you the strength to wipe away your tears, hold on to it for dear life and nurture it with all your heart. Because at the end of the day, your money, your job, your career, and all of those Oblivions who tried to keep you down won't be following you into the afterlife.

The love you've left behind will be the energy that propels you to your next journey.

BACK TO THE BASICS

As far as beauty and personal hygiene products go, I think I've tried them all.

I'm talking thousands of dollars over the past decade on various shaving creams, aftershaves, deodorants, colognes, lotions, soaps, hair gels, shampoos, stick wax, and overpriced haircuts.

Never once did I emerge from my bathroom looking like Joe Millionaire.

Several years ago I gave up trying so hard to look good. I abandoned the expensive stuff and have adopted what my father's been using for as long as I can remember—Old Spice. It's cheap, it smells good, and it's reliable. But there's something deeper than just being frugal that motivates me.

One of my fondest memories from my childhood is when I would watch my father shave every morning before he went to work as a UPS man. It was an artistic ritual of careful precision that would end with a splash of that cool, brisk aftershave on his face. I used to love how the scent lingered in the bathroom all morning. Somewhere on the road between childhood and adulthood I lost my way.

I discovered designer brands in college. There, some of my so-called friends wouldn't don a shirt unless it had a guy riding a horse on it. I followed the pack. I started using expensive cologne, bought those shirts, and somehow ended up with a regular $50 buzz cut from a hoity-toity "beauty salon." After college I continued on this pampered endeavor for years, hopping from one Manhattan salon bearing a Frenchman's name to another, each one a little more expensive than the last. The trend continued until September 11, 2001.

On that horrible day I realized that my wife, my family, my country, my friends, and even my pets were more important to me than anything else in the world. And I felt foolish for being so vain all those years. I don't think I was any kind of a monster, but what kind of a moron would spend more than sixty bucks, plus tip, on a buzz cut? What idiot buys $40 shaving cream and $60 aftershave? Or a $200 nickel-plated "shaving utensil"? Me. Despite all the pampering, I didn't like what I saw in the mirror (and my father likes to joke that I've never seen a mirror that I didn't like).

But it had nothing to do with the image that I could see. It had to do with the one that's harder to see. The one that only the people who truly love you can see but who never tell you just how bad a sight it is.

So now I use Old Spice aftershave, soap, and deodorant. I go to a barber for my $10 buzz. I've abandoned the overcrowded and overpriced gym for the home-based Bowflex. I save money, and I'm not so image-conscious. I am not alone. Men across the country are liberated in the sense that the days of the '90s sensitive man in touch with his feminine side are gone. The man of the new millennium combines the sensitivity that women cherish with the machismo women want.

Being in the TV business, I still need to make a conscientious effort to try to look good. But as I get older, I realize the message is more important than the messenger. These days I concentrate more on what I'm saying or writing, rather than how I look doing it.

The World's Biggest Oblivions

THE 911 DRIVE-THRU WOMAN

Sometimes Oblivions are just too good to be true. Take for instance, the California woman who dialed 911 from a Burger King drive-thru because the staff didn't make her hamburger the way she wanted.

You can't make this stuff up folks. Here's the transcript from the San Clemente Sheriff's office:

Dispatcher: Sheriff's Department, how can I help you?

Oblivion: Yeah, I'm over here . . . I'm over here at Burger King right here in San Clemente.

Dispatcher: Uh-huh.

Oblivion: Um, no, not San Clemente; I'm sorry, I live in San Clemente. I'm in Laguna Niguel, I think, that's where I'm at.

Dispatcher: Uh-huh.

Oblivion: I'm at a drive-thru right now.

Dispatcher: Uh-huh.

Oblivion: I went . . . I ordered my food *three* times. They're mopping the floor inside, and I understand they're
busy. . . . They're not even busy, okay, I've been the
only car here. I asked them *four* different times to make
me a Western Barbeque Burger. Okay, they keep giving
me a hamburger with lettuce, tomato, and cheese,
onions, and I said, "I'm not leaving . . ."

Dispatcher: Uh-huh.

Oblivion: I want a Western Burger because I just got my kids
from Tae Kwon Do, they're hungry, I'm on my way
home, and I live in San Clemente.

Dispatcher: Uh-huh.

Oblivion: Okay . . . she said, she gave me another hamburger; it's
wrong. I said *four* times, I said, "I want it to go." "Can
you go out and park in front?" I said, "No, I want my
hamburger right." So then the . . . the lady came to the
manager. She . . . well, whoever she is, she came up
and she said, um, she said, um, "Do you want your
money back?" And I said, "No, I want my hamburger.
My kids are hungry and I have to jump on that toll
freeway." I said, "I am not leaving this spot," and I
said, "I will call the police," because I want my Western Burger done right! Now is that so hard?

Dispatcher: Okay, what exactly is it you want us to do for you?

Oblivion: I . . . send an officer down here. I . . . I want them to make me—

Dispatcher: Ma'am, we're not gonna go down there and enforce your Western Bacon Cheeseburger.

Oblivion: What am I supposed to do?

Dispatcher: This is . . . this is between you and the manager. We're not gonna go and enforce how to make a hamburger; that's not a criminal issue. There's . . . there's nothing criminal there.

Oblivion: So I just stand here . . . so I just sit here and [block]?

Dispatcher: You . . . you need to calmly and rationally speak to the manager and figure out what to do between you.

Oblivion: She did come up, and I said, "Can I please have my Western Burger?" She . . . she said, "I'm not dealing with it," and she walked away. Because they're mopping the floor, and it's also the fact that they don't want to . . . they don't want to go through there . . . and . . . and . .

Dispatcher: Ma'am, then I suggest you get your money back and go somewhere else. This is . . . this is not a criminal issue. We can't go out there and make them make you a cheeseburger the way you want it.

Oblivion: Well . . . that is . . . that . . . you're supposed to be here to protect me.

Dispatcher: Well, what are we protecting you from, a wrong cheeseburger?

Oblivion: No . . .

Dispatcher: Is this like . . . is this a harmful cheeseburger or something? I don't understand what you want us to do.

Oblivion: Just come down here. I'm not . . . I'm not leaving.

Dispatcher: No ma'am, I'm not sending the deputies down there over a cheeseburger. You need to go in there and act like an adult and either get your money back or go home.

Oblivion: She is not acting like an adult herself! I'm sitting here in my car; I just want them to make my kids a . . . a Western Burger.

Dispatcher: Ma'am, this is what I suggest: I suggest you get your money back from the manager and you go on your way home.

Oblivion: Okay.

Dispatcher: Okay? Bye-bye.

MICHAEL MOORE

This guy has the biggest mouth on the face of the planet, and he's a worse propagandist than even your most hated politician. Moore calls himself a "filmmaker," even though he shoots on tape, not film. Moore calls himself a champion of the blue collar people, specifically his union-loving *Roger and Me*, meanwhile all of his productions use non-union crews, in a production industry where the unions are everywhere.

Michael Moore ambushed Charlton Heston in order to make a point in his film *Bowling For Columbine*. Heston opened his door to Moore, probably because he was already suffering from Alzeimer's disease, and Moore goes in and blasts him for being the president of the NRA, all for the sake of his "film."

In my opinion, he would use the same kinds of tactics in his next and most successful documentary, *Fahrenheit 9/11*—which grossed $220 million worldwide.

In it, Moore inserted interviews shot by a freelance crew in Iraq with an adrenaline-fueled tank regiment who were rolling into battle with the Iraqis.

The last thing these guys were concerned with as they headed into parts unknown was being politically correct, something that, had they had even a tenth of the training they had in killing the enemy in say, Media 101, they would have surely been very aware of.

In my view, Mr. Moore took advantage of the naiveté of those soldiers, much the same way TV-anchor-turned-lounge-act Connie Chung took advantage of Newt Gingrich's mom in an interview where Chung told Kathy Gingrich that anything she said about First Lady Hillary Rodham-Clinton would stay between them.

Newt's mom went on to say that her boy, then the Speaker of the House, says he thinks "Hillary's a bitch." Needless to say, Chung didn't keep the remarks private.

Yup, Michael Moore has the same journalistic integrity as Mrs. Maury Povich.

But like Chung, Moore got what he needed in order to tell the story he wanted to tell, the story about how big, bad America is attacking poor, innocent Iraq.

Incidentally, in May 2006, Sgt. Peter Damon, a National Guardsman who lost both his arms when a tire on a Black Hawk helicopter he was servicing exploded, sued Moore, Disney, and NBC News for nearly $200 million in damages, claiming "defamation and inflicting of emotional distress."

Damon agreed to be interviewed by NBC *Nightly News*, where he said that he felt like he was being "crushed like a vice." That interview, with Damon lying on a stretcher, appeared in *9/11*, edited to make it look like Damon was antiwar, an assertion the armless soldier refutes wholeheartedly.

"I don't regret going to Iraq at all. I'm very proud of my service," Damon told the FOX owned and operated station WFXT in Boston.

From just these two examples, you can see how easy it is for any person with an editor to make anything fit nicely into an agenda.

For me the most Grrring part of *9/11* was when Moore cut scenes from that fateful day in New York City in slow motion, over ominous music and in pitch black screens, giving the impression to the viewer that the people in those buildings got what they deserved.

Then he cuts to Iraqi children playing soccer and Iraqi women looking lovingly at them, and then cuts to the bombing campaign that marked the beginning of the war. Big bad America hurting the innocents of the world.

Forget politics for a minute. Forget whether or not you believe we should have ever gone into Iraq, or if you think we should have gone more "shock and awe."

What did those innocent, mostly multinational citizens who were blown up, burned alive, suffocated, crushed to death, or who decided to take fate into their own hands and jump from one hundred stories high at the World Trade Center ever do to Michael Moore?

Didn't the families of those innocent Americans who perished deserve the same opportunity to grieve or express their hurt in Moore's movie, as he afforded the Iraqis who appeared, equipped with subtitles, to express their pain?

Absolutely. But that would have brought sympathy to our victims, something Moore wasn't really interested in, because his agenda was to make President Bush look bad, and to hell with the victims and their families.

Moore had a story he wanted to tell. A story that in the end, he knew would play well overseas, one that would net him more money than any other movie he's ever made.

That, in my opinion, is what Moore is really all about.

ANN COULTER

With her 2006 book *Godless,* conservative political pundit Ann Coulter jumped the shark. Why?

Coulter went too far when she called a group of 9/11 windows "harpies" who seem to be "enjoying their husbands' deaths" in her new book. She even added: "And by the way, how do we know their husbands weren't planning to divorce these harpies? Now that their shelf life is dwindling, they'd better hurry up and appear in *Playboy....*"

Huh?

Ugly is the only way I can describe what Coulter had written. Now I understand why *Time* magazine put her on the cover in the summer of 2005 and made her look like a praying mantis. She just might be the type of creature that would eat its mate after sex.

Coulter's comments would be more understandable if they had been off-the-cuff remarks on some television show. After all, she is known for shooting off about liberals and anybody else who questions the Bush administration. At least then her remarks would have only been heard on that one show, and if there was a backlash she could have chalked it up to a misunderstanding—which by the way, there wasn't. At least with her fans.

But these abhorrent comments were written in a book. Books don't just hit the printing press as soon as authors submit them to a publisher. They are edited. They are read by marketing executives, agents, and editors.

Surely somebody at Crown Forum, the publishing house behind Coulter's inflammatory tome, must have read these paragraphs and questioned whether they shouldn't just be deleted.

It was probably some marketing genius who fought to keep the words intact. "Imagine the outrage and subsequent book sales," he might have said. In the end, that's what it's all about, isn't it? Money.

Book sales, appearances on the *Today* show, radio shows, more outlets to syndicate her column, and her next book deal might be what Coulter was thinking about when she pecked at her keyboard and formed such ill-conceived thoughts.

As all commentators, writers, talk-show hosts, experts, and pundits with any type of national or local platform know, you must have an audience if you want to continue to make a living in media.

Sometimes commentator-types simply pander to their audience—and sometimes the things they say are utterly unchallenging and frankly insulting to that audience, no matter who they are.

I can't tell you how many times I've written something that I believed wholeheartedly to be true, but recognized the comments were mean spirited and may have gone too far for the sake of going too far. I deleted them. There are more words about Paris Hilton in my computer trash bin than you might even imagine.

Also, I don't know that any educated, conservative-minded person (Coulter's target demographic) would really want to hear *speculation* about the marital status of people who were involved in the worst terrorist attack on our nation's soil.

Coulter should have known her remarks would cause controversy. But she may have underestimated how sensitive even her own audience might be to such an ignorant rant.

THE CORPORATE ROBBER BARONS

People like Enron's Jeffrey Skilling and Ken Lay, Worldcom's Bernie Ebbers, and Tyco's Dennis Kozlowski were just despicable when it came to their greed. They are no better than the John Gottis and Joey Merlinos of the mob world. On one hand they gave a lot of money to charities. In fact, Merlino was once described as a modern-day Robin Hood. But as one federal agent told *The Philadelphia Inquirer* journalist George Anastasia about Merlino: "It's easy to give money away when it's not your money to begin with."

Many hard-working people lost their jobs because these CEOs were out for themselves, living the most lavish lifestyles normal people couldn't begin to fathom. When is enough enough? Have they no shame?

Sadly, no.

JON STEWART

I have a lot of respect for Stewart, but when did his comedy show become a mouthpiece against the Republican Party? To be fair, Stewart skewered the Clinton administration, too, but in the George W. Bush heydays, Stewart went for the jugular more often than the laugh.

Of course, it was funny when he lambasted Paul Begala and Tucker Carlson on their CNN snoozefest *Crossfire*, but who the hell does Jon Stewart think he is, anyway? Oprah Winfrey?

The thing is, I'd like to have the following as my defense every time somebody criticizes me: "The lead-in to my program is a show with puppets making crank calls."

This is supposed to disarm his critics with the notion that he is simply a comedian on a network that doesn't really matter. It may be a fact that his show falls under the comedy and parody categories, but the truth is *The Daily Show* is important, and long ago blurred the line between truth and fiction.

For this, I blame those print reporters who cover the television industry, who fawn over the brilliance of Stewart and his staff of producers and writers. These are the same people who anointed *Saturday Night Live's* former head writer and *Weekend Update* coanchor Tina Fey the funniest and most brilliant female ever to grace the small screen.

Why do you think print journalists pick comedians who are playing the role of TV anchor, while making fun of the real TV anchors, on shows that fall under the comedy and parody categories?

Because Jon Stewart and Tina Fey get to say in "jest," exactly what the print reporters would love to say seriously. But these reporters know darn well that they'll be shut out from access to the stars and network executives they need to interview for their own careers to continue to flourish.

Stewart and Fey are their mouthpieces. The problem with Stewart, I think, is that he believes his own press, and as self-deprecating and funny and talented as he is, there are times when he just goes too far with his holier-than-thou act.

And let's not forget folks, that it is an act. Well, when it's convenient. Puppets, remember?

But hey Jon, don't mind me.

After all, I write the "Grrr!" column. You can't take anyone who uses onomatopoeia so often and in the title of his work, and who makes up his own words, too seriously.

OPRAH WINFREY

Here is a woman who has worked her way up the ranks to become the most powerful woman in America. God bless her.

But the audience still has the power to sway her.

Take the time she was upset that Hermès in Paris refused to let her in after the store had closed. The clerk obviously didn't know who Oprah Winfrey was, and therefore Oprah was pissed. She made statements about how she would address the issue when her television program came back after hiatus.

But when the much anticipated episode aired, and Winfrey interviewed the president of Hermès, North America, the queen of daytime television actually endorsed Hermès's overpriced Berkin bag, saying that even though she was snubbed, everybody should have one. Huh? I was half expecting a bunch of production assistants to start handing out $20,000 handbags to all of the women in the audience as punishment to the boutique firm, much like the time she gave away Pontiacs and stuck her studio audience with the tax bills.

But she didn't. That was that. After months of waiting for the Great & Powerful Oprah to bring down the hammer, nada. Zilch.

Instead, Oprah saved all of the venom for liar-turned-author James Frey, for duping her into endorsing his drug-rehab "memoir" *A Million Little Pieces,* which turned out to be chock-full of lies and exaggerations. Oprah beat him to a pulp along with his Doubleday publisher, Nan Talese, and I was with her all the way, until she started pointing fingers at the publishing world and demanding that they change the way they do business.

"Things have to change in the industry," she said.

Hah! That's laughable coming from someone who makes her living in daytime television—not that she's Jerry Springer, mind you. But, perhaps we should go back and look at every single one of her programs and decide which guest wasn't really molested as a child but just happened to tell a great story to get on television? Which guest wasn't really beaten by her husband? Which guest was actually a very good parent, but played the Deadbeat Dad role just to be on TV?

The reason the Queen of Daytime Television treated the Hermès and Frey incidents so differently was because in the case of Hermès,

Oprah knew that her public would be outraged if she believed she deserved "special treatment" because she's a celebrity. After all of the facts came out, it was established that the store in Paris was closed for a private event.

After no doubt consulting with her producers and public relations experts, Oprah probably realized she was damned if she did beat up Hermès, and damned if she didn't!

In Frey's case, Oprah went on national television to defend him, and after receiving thousands of e-mails condemning her for essentially saying the truth was not important, she flip-flopped on Frey and burned him big-time. In short, she saved her own skin by burning his, but took a temporary hit on her credibility.

In August of 2006 Oprah made yet another error in judgement and overestimated her star power.

In her own magazine O, Ms. Winfrey felt the need to dispel rumors that she and best friend Gayle King, the editor-in-chief of O, were in fact, not lesbians, and she wrote an editorial explaining a relationship that "feels otherworldly," but that most people couldn't understand.

Oprah took a beating in the public arena for that one, and once again it seemed like the gloves were coming off against the undisputed champ.

What, did Oprah hire Tom Cruise's sister, Leann Devitt, as an advisor that year? Because it sure seemed that Winfrey made as many public blunders as her favorite couch jumping movie star did after he fired his longtime publicist, Pat Kingsley.

Is any of this earth-shattering? No. Is it Oblivionism? Yup.

JENNIFER WILBANKS: RUNAWAY BRIDE

Remember the "fleeancée" who disappeared a week before her Georgia wedding without so much as a word to the people who care about her?

Apparently Jennifer Wilbanks planned her escape from the altar, purchasing her bus ticket and cutting her hair in advance, as well as setting cash aside for her journey across the country. Much was made of Wilbanks's mental state, but this doesn't sound like someone who was acting on the spur of the moment or was under undue stress.

Once she ran out of money in Albuquerque, New Mexico, she concocted a kidnapping story. She said a Hispanic man and a white woman abducted her and raped her, but quickly came clean when she realized that cops are actually pretty smart when they want to be.

Duluth, Georgia, mayor Shirley Lassetter estimated the cost of the search for Wilbanks to have been around $100,000, but that doesn't include the diner and restaurant owners who donated coffee and food to those involved in the search, and who knows how many other caring small-business owners who may have given away merchandise to prepare volunteers for the search.

Wilbanks was obviously distressed. But haven't we all been "in crisis," at one time or another? Doesn't mean we'd do something so incredibly self-centered and irresponsible.

JANE FONDA

Somebody gag me with a spoon. A tablespoon. No, make it a ladle. Ah, hell, why not throw the whole pot down my throat. Am I the only one sick of hearing about how hard a life poor little Jane Fonda had at the hands of her emotionally distant movie-star daddy?

Oh boo hoo hoo!

Did poor Barbarella Arnold, a.k.a. Hanoi Jane, suffer the demons of the neglected little rich girl, starved so much for attention that she engaged in sex with prostitutes, took part in orgies, and hid her Christian faith from all of the abusive men in her life?

Of course, she saves all this trauma for when her book tour is in full swing and in appearances on everything from *60 Minutes* to *Good Morning America,* all in the name of selling a book and making even more money, than her poor, poor, sad life had already seen.

But "Oh, she's so brave for telling us her problems." Yeah, methinks we are seeing the prelude to the Paris Hilton of year 2040.

But wait, there's more.

All of the publicity happened just as her "big Hollywood comeback" movie, *Monster-in-Law,* with Ms. Box-Office Flop herself, Jennifer Lopez, came out. Another little convenient fact.

FORMER N.J. GOVERNOR JIM MCGREEVEY

Where were you on April 20, 2004, when New Jersey Governor James McGreevey held a surprise news conference where he announced to the world that he had had an extramarital affair—with a male employee?

I was standing in a newsroom, and as jaded as journalists are, there was a collective gasp among the hundreds of staffers who were glued to their desktop TV sets.

Suddenly the place erupted with action, and the news cycle just had its new lead story. While I can understand the subsequent media frenzy, I couldn't help but be Grrred over McGreevey's use of the term he used to come out of the closet:

"Gay American."

The term, which was also reportedly the working title of his memoir, *The Confession,* inspired me to write this column about my own inner conflict, and it relieved me of my anguish.

A Bombshell Announcement

For years now I've been fooling myself, although I probably wasn't fooling anyone around me.

I walked through the newsroom or attended social gatherings with family and friends with complete confidence in who I am. I've stood *tall* among my peers. I've accomplished things.

It wasn't until New Jersey Governor James McGreevey held his shocking national press conference that I began to have doubts about my true identity. Finally, the time has come. It is with great pride that I announce . . . that I am a short American.

That's right. I'm about five feet six and a half inches tall. I'll admit that sometimes when I'm conducting red carpet interviews with celebrities I will wear boots that make me about five feet eight inches tall. It makes my cameraman's job easier when it comes to framing the two-shot.

I know that this bombshell announcement will rock the "Grrr!" readership to its core, but alas, I had to do it.

Now, obviously I'm joking (not about being short, but about the "bombshell announcement"). But am I the only person Grrred about the use of the word *American* when people use it in a way to try to gain sympathy from society and deflect from the real issue?

"I am a gay American." "I am a straight American." "I am a black American." "I am a white American." "I am a short American." "I am a whatever American."

The intent of the use of the word *American* is along the lines of "Don't judge me poorly, because I, just like you, am an American."

Give me a break.

Does that mean convicts should come out of prison to announce they are "criminal Americans"? Will that make you feel better about renting them an apartment or hiring them for employment? Or how about "I am a terrorist American"? Taliban Johnny could have used that in his defense. Reality-show contestants can be "reality Americans."

In the case of Governor McGreevey, "I am a liar American" would have been more appropriate.

Imagine if he came out to say that he had been having an affair with a woman he hired to be New Jersey's homeland security chief—not because she was qualified, but because he was having an affair with her. He'd be vilified by women's groups. He'd be labeled a dirtbag adulterer—not a tragic homosexual figure.

Instead, he's a "gay American," thus implying he's dealing with something more than just being a dirtbag. Are we supposed to think, *Poor guy, must have been tortured living such a lie for so long?* Well, yes, actually. It's what his focus groups probably told him we would feel before he made his "spontaneous" bombshell announcement.

Hey, better to come out as a "gay American" dealing with a burden than to be thought of as an adulterer who uses his power to award high-paying jobs to his lover—gay or straight.

COREY CLARK

Remember the ABC News exposé on what they called an "explosive sex scandal behind the scenes at *American Idol*"?

Whether or not you think Paula Abdul should have exited the show—as I did at the time—after allegations she had a conflict-of-interest affair with Corey Clark, a season-two reject, you still have to admire her guts, if not her judgement.

Like so many other celebrities caught in a scandal, she could have checked into rehab and taken the sympathy route. She didn't.

But I have four major Grrrs about the whole Abdul/Clark affair.

1. Grrr! on ABC's Primetime for airing this so-called "exposé" on the scandal behind the scenes at a rival network's No. 1 rated show.

What's next in TV news? Will *60 Minutes* do a story about Botox use on *Desperate Housewives*? Or should all network news divisions do exposés on Disneyland?

Surely, Disney-owned ABC News could have reported Clark's claims without promoting his CD or his family's band, and they could have taken these allegations with a grain of salt, couldn't they?

Instead, they opened the hour-long report with Clark singing a tune from his CD. Moreover, they brushed over Clark's arrests for assault and passing bad checks, taking Clark's word that he was wrongfully arrested, but never airing an interview with one of the four arresting officers or the prosecutor in the case.

They showed phone records with incoming calls from Abdul's home number, but never reported whether they verified that the calls indeed came from Abdul herself.

They mention a Sprint employee who witnessed Abdul buying a cell phone for Clark but never aired an interview with said employee. They produced a cash receipt for clothes, taking Clark's word that Abdul paid for them, and the only corroborating witnesses who saw Abdul and Clark together were Clark's buddies.

Hardly the stuff of investigative reporting.

2. Grrr! on Paula Abdul for staying silent and for appearing on Saturday Night Live *in a sketch about her predicament.*

We know *AI* is not saving lives here, but it is a worldwide phenomenon that should have utmost integrity and should be taken seriously by the people profiting the most from it, especially Abdul. If all of the above is so untrue, how come she didn't come out and state that fact firmly herself, instead of issuing weak statements through her personal attorneys?

3. Grrr! on SNL for brushing over the allegations and letting Abdul off the hook so easily.

Can you imagine if Simon Cowell were in a similar predicament? I'm sure "Weekend Update" coanchor at the time Tina Fey would have been reporting over and over about how horrible a person Cowell is, like she does when other famous men are accused of sexual harassment. But when a famous woman is caught red-handed, that's okay.

4. If Clark was telling the truth, Grrr! to him for using Abdul's lack of judgment for his own personal gain.

He kept saying he didn't want to hurt her, then went on Howard Stern and aired all the lurid details about how he remembered the alleged affair—and he didn't spare anything, folks. On top of all the kissing and telling, this ignoramus went on to say that "a credible source, an AP story," was reporting that Abdul's and his phone calls were being monitored by the FBI under the PATRIOT Act because Abdul had the same name as a wanted terrorist.

The "credible story" this idiot was referring to was a satire written by Deanna Swift of *The Swift Report* blogs, which is truly a funny piece of satire but hardly a credible source. It only shows just what kind of fool we're dealing with here.

Corey, if you're such a good singer, you could have made it without all of this. If you were a man, you would have. In my book, you're nothing but a little bitch. Tell that to ABC News.

FAN MAIL

The "Grrr!" column gets it fair share of e-mail. It's funny how the same column can be read and interpreted so differently by so many people. Here are a few items I've received throughout the years. Enjoy.

Ghosty1 writes: "Mike, you never keep your mouth shut! You are a professional bitch columnist! Not only that, but you choose as your column name, the cutting, intriguing name of GRRRR. Get a new schtick, PLEASE!"

Patrick N. writes: "Straka, You really crack me up! I, for one, really appreciate your powers of observance and your ability to put it all down on paper, so to speak! A lot of times, you articulate what the rest of us only WISH we could put into words when it comes to the Obliviots of the world!"

Thomas C. writes: "I'm surprised you didn't need to pay for an extra ticket on the plane to accommodate your ego. In case you hadn't been paying attention in astronomy class, the world does not, in fact, revolve around you. . . . You are the living excrement of society."

Greg B. writes: "Wonderful how you put things in perspective and it's funny too. Keep at it now matter how much slack you get."

Eddie B. writes: "You must have written this out of your ass, it stinks!"

Sam G. writes: "Mike: Finally!! I can assure you that there are millions of people in this country that agree with you 100 percent, including me. I can also assure you that there are people reading your article, agreeing with it, and they're on the list and don't know it; hence Oblivions."

Jim J. writes: "The Grrr! Lexicon is Outstanding! The only problem, Mike, is, these kinds of people probably don't read your stuff, do they? I sure wish I could figure out a way do something about these behaviors, but I don't think it's possible really."

Dan M. answers my letter to the Oblivion Council: "We are in receipt of your recent inquiry for membership. Due to overwhelming interest we currently allow only purists on 'The List' you mentioned. Please be informed that our organization's bylaws do not allow or permit any of its members to operate in any manner other than in complete transparency, and any assertion otherwise will result in the immediate suspension of your application. Keeping in accordance with policy, your application will be reviewed at a later date, and at that time, we will contact you directly for an interview."

Bruce F. writes: "My words of 'Grrr!' wisdom: 1. Always read the

'Grrr!' column. 2. Memorize the 'Grrr!' Lexicon. 3. NEVER sit next to Mike Straka on an airplane."

Jessica W. writes: "AWESOME! Someone in the media is finally saying how I feel!"

Jen M. writes: "Why are you so angry at the world? Get a grip . . . and some Xanax."

John W. writes: "According to you everyone but yourself has something severely wrong with them. Yes, sometimes you do admit to doing the things you Grrr about, but you admit to it in a way where it was necessary or you weren't thinking clearly. Whatever. I'll tell you what you are, you're one of those guys that spends too much time observing how others act and react to the point that it makes you sick and have to spew your words all over the Internet . . . although, I do like your column."

Dean Humphrey writes: "Saw you pulling anchor duties and was impressed. You are not just some grumpy curmudgeon like me. As a side note, I always enjoy when you tell little tales about celebrities you've come across. Kudos for all your work."

Dave Chen writes: "Thank you so much for being the voice of reason in this confusing time. I'm glad to read that not everyone in the media agrees with the minority and the majority opinion is still being heard. Keep the dialogue alive."

Larry W. writes: "You need to lay off the sauce (at least during the day). Funny and biting—even the delusional parts."

Paul Y. writes: "You disgust me! Your column is not funny and I think they should refuse to publish anymore of your repugnant trash! GO TO HELL!"

$(((\ldots)))$

Epilogue

As you can see, I'm plagued by Oblivions everyday. I know it seems like I am an angry young man, but believe it or not, I'm not. That's because Grrring is extremely therapeutic. You should try it sometime. It will add years to your life because you won't be so stressed.

Like I said in the beginning, Oblivions have been around for thousands of years, and they're not going anywhere. We just have to learn to live with them and occassionally we have to teach them how not to be Oblivions.

Hopefully this book will help, but of course all of the Oblivions who are reading these pages now were nodding in agreement all along, and they don't even know that I was Grrring them.

ACKNOWLEDGMENTS

Thanks to Elizabeth and Frank, my mom and dad, who have always been there when I need them and who have been great friends and supporters, and to my sister Melissa and my brother-in-law Joe, who are great friends. Thanks also to my big brother Frankie, and to Jack and Ann Straw, the in-laws, for their support.

This book would not have been possible without the following people, from those who pushed me to go for it, to those who helped craft my style, and those who okayed it.

My bosses at FOX News Channel, especially Bert Solivan and Dianne Brandi, for saying yes when the book came about, and of course, Mr. Ailes, the CEO and Chairman of FOX News, who has been an inspiration to everybody in our building.

Thanks to Marc Resnick at St. Martins Press who took a chance on me and the Grrr!, Rebecca Heller at St. Martin's for all her help, Ian Kleinert, my agent at the Literary Group, and Rob Cea, a talented writer, producer, and, as it turns out, a great pitchman.

But most important are the "Grrr!" readers who read the column and email "Your Grrrs" every week, and who have been asking for a "Grrr!" book for a long time. Thank you for your support.

FOX News has always given me enough rope to hang myself with, but Bert and everybody else at the shop, including the entire second floor executive suite, usually catch me at just the right moment.

So thanks to Mark Kranz, John Moody, Bill Shine, Kevin Magee, Rich O'Brien, Joe Chillemi, John Stack, Sharri Berg, Maureen Hunt, Janet Alshouse (who hired me), Jack Abernethy, Tim Carry, John Malkin, Chris Silvestri, Lesley West, Bob Finnerty, Mitch Davis, Brian Jones, Doug Murphy, Judith Slater, Roger Domal, Paul Rittenberg, Jeremy Steinberg, Brian Lewis, Irene Briganti, Dan Klinghoffer, Diana Rocco, and especially Suzanne Scott and Joe Maline, who have always been supportive and whose advice I seek often.

A special thanks to Warren Vandeveer and David Winstrom, for believing in me and serving up the big projects that helped me get noticed, and Marvin Himelfarb, the bravest man in television. Thanks for putting me out there and getting me some great assignments.

To the editors at FOXNews.com who shape the "Grrr!" column every week, Refet Kaplan, Robin Wallace, and Marla Lehner, who were there in the beginning, to Jen D'Angelo who edits it every week, thank you for looking out for me all of these years.

Thanks to Steve Bromberg, the executive editor at FOXNews.com, who saves my butt week in and week out. When writing a column like "Grrr!," making mistakes is not an option, and Steve has helped keep me credible.

I would also like to thank all of the photogs, from Tommy Chiu and crew chief Janette Shaw and everyone else in the field, who have made me look good all of these years, and the FOX editing and promos departments, who put everything together just right, especially *The Real Deal* Nancy Foster and the *Keeping It Reel* gurus Matt Riggs and Jason Ehrich.

And over at that other shop where I used to work, Les Moonves has always been an inspiration, Harry Dank at CBS News was a good mentor and a better journalist, and Joe Long and Andy Rothman, it's always fun to run into you guys out on those shoots, especially when you're trying to steal my guests. Just kidding.

Thanks to all of you who contributed blurbs for the book. I am truly thankful and humbled.

Also, a giant thanks to copy editor Mark Steven Long, whose line edit of this book forced me to rework a lot of my thoughts, and made me a better writer in the process.

I know that there are several others I left out, so suffice it to say that I thank everybody whom I've worked with and whose talents I've relied on all of these years, as we help each other and challenge each other to be better and better, every day.

And to my best buds Greg, Claus, Dave, Tony, and Joe, you guys are lasting friends who mean the world to me.